The Forgotten Option

The Forgotten Option

A place of growth between marriage and divorce

Kenneth Connelly

gatekeeper press

Columbus, Ohio

Scripture Permissions

NIV [New International Version]

Scriptures are taken from the Holy Bible, New International Version, NIV. Copyright 1973, 1978, 1984, 2011 by Biblica, Inc.™ Used by permission of Zondervan. All rights reserved worldwide. www.Zondervan.com The "NIV" and "New International Version" are trademarks registered in the United States Patent and Trademark Office by Biblica, Inc.™

ESV [English Standard Version]

Scripture quotations are taken from the ESV Bible (The HolyBible, English Standard Version), copyright 2001 by Crossway, a publishing ministry of Good News Publishers. Used by permission. All rights reserved.

NLT [New Living Translation]

Scripture quotations marked [NLT/New Living Translation] are taken from the Holy Bible, New Living Translation, copyright 1996, 2004, 2015 by Tyndale House Foundation. Used by permission of Tyndale House Publishers, a Division of Tyndale House Ministries, Carol Stream, Illinois 60188. All rights reserved.

MEV [Modern English Version]

Scripture quotations are taken from the Modern English Version, copyright 2014 by Military Bible Association. Used by permission. All rights reserved.

The Forgotten Option: A place of growth between marriage and divorce

Published by Gatekeeper Press
2167 Stringtown Rd, Suite 109
Columbus, OH 43123-2989
www.GatekeeperPress.com

The cover design, interior formatting, typesetting, and editorial work for this book are entirely the product of the author. Gatekeeper Press did not participate in and is not responsible for any aspect of these elements.

ISBN (hardcover): 9781662901034
ISBN (paperback): 9781662901041
eISBN: 9781662901058

Library of Congress Control Number: 2020940228

'Better the end of a thing than its beginning; and the patient in spirit is better than a proud in spirit.'

Solomon
Ecclesiastes 7:8
English Standard Version

To Cindy
For your influence in my life

Contents

Forward

I have just finished reading The Forgotten Option. Being that it is Ken's first work, I am very impressed.

This book takes a very honest and up front look at, what is in our society, the too easy option of divorce. As one who has been married since 1975 to the same woman, who has worked in the field of marriage and family therapy since 2000, and who has counseled many couples before marriage and hundreds after they said "I do", I encourage you to read this book. I say this all the more if you are having problems in your marriage and are considering divorce; do so before you give up on your marriage and see the lawyers.

I am so thankful for the fact that after two and a half years of marriage, when I was abusive in my marriage, that my wife did not leave me – even though she wanted to. Instead, she agreed to stay and go with me to counseling, which changed our marriage and subsequently our lives forever. Now as I write, having been married for 45 years, I have three adult children, 14 grandchildren and 1 great grand-daughter. I am thankful for the commitment my wife showed when she could have given up on me and our marriage. I am thankful for our mutual willingness to hang in there.

There may be a time for divorce, but too often it is the first thought that enters into a person's mind when there is fight, after fight, after fight - or worse. This information that Ken has thoughtfully written, from his own experience and wisdom of his years, gives you food for thought in The Forgotten Option. I hope you will slow down and consider carefully The Forgotten Option before you end the marriage with divorce.

Please read this and apply what is written here. And also, please, please - pass it on to someone you know who may be considering divorce. Who knows? It may save generations from the pains of divorce that are so deep, words cannot describe.

Reverend Dr. Marcial Felan
Licensed Marriage & Family Therapist
La Mesa, CA

The Front Cover

On the front cover of this book are some kids on a beach, looking down among the rocks on the shore, intent in their pursuit of finding something. What they're trying to find with such intensity on this day, I'm not sure of. From their well-kept dress, the location, and their ability to be so carefree - I am assuming they are not alone. Somewhere outside of this photograph is most likely a dad and a mom, maybe a grandparent or two as well, watching over their growth and maturity with care. If this is not the case, it should be. And though they may not know it, there is a Father above that loves them with a fierce love too. Teenagers, kids, society and families – they all are part of my inspiration for writing this.

⌇

I want to pull an excerpt from a profound and insightful book that was written on the effects of divorce.[1] It not only has to do with these young people on the cover, but my kids, my grandkids, all of yours too, and every other child that came into the world needing love.

The author writes,

'Two faulty beliefs provide the foundation for our current attitudes toward divorce. The first holds *that if the parents are happier the children will be happier, too.* Even if the children are distressed by the divorce, the crisis will be transient because the children are resilient and resourceful and will soon recover.

A second myth is based on the premise *that divorce is a temporary crisis that exerts its most harmful effects on parents and children at the time of the breakup.* The belief that the crisis is temporary underlies the notion that if acceptable legal arrangements for custody, visiting, and child support are made at the time of the divorce and parents are provided with a few lectures, the child will soon be fine. It is a view we have fervently embraced and continue to hold. *But it's misguided.*

Adult children of divorce are telling us loud and clear their parent's anger at the time of the breakup is not what matters most. Unless there was violence or abuse or unremitting high conflict, *they have dim memories of what transpired during this supposedly critical period.* Indeed, as youngsters then and as adults now, all would be profoundly astonished to learn that any judge, attorney, mediator – indeed, anyone at all – had genuinely considered their best interests or wishes at the breakup or any time since. It's the many years living in a post-divorce or remarried family that count, according to this first generation to come of age and tell us their experience. It's feeling sad, lonely, and angry during childhood. It's traveling on airplanes alone when you're seven to visit your parent. It's having no choice about how you spend your time and feeling like a second-class citizen compared with your friends in intact families who have some say about how they spend their weekends and their vacations. It's wondering whether you will have any financial help for college from your college-educated father, given that he has no legal obligation to pay. It's worrying about your mom and dad for years – will her new boyfriend stick around, will his new wife welcome you into her home? It's reaching adulthood with acute anxiety. Will you ever find a faithful woman to love you? Will you find a man you can trust? Or will your relationships fail just like you parents did? And most tellingly, it's asking if you can protect your own child from having these same experiences in growing up.

Not one of the men or women from divorced families whose lives I report on in this book wanted their children to repeat their childhood experiences. Not one ever said, "I want my children to live in two nests – or even two villas." They envied friends who grew up in intact families. Their entire life stories belie the myths we've embraced.'

~~

So these aren't just teenagers or kids, whether they are yours or mine. These children represent the reason why we should consider options that return us to commitment – to not call it quits and walk away.

Even if you don't have young ones yet, or never will, still there is a tight bond to marriage that shouldn't be broken. It is to this hopeful end of a lasting marriage that I ultimately want to guide us all, in the best way that I know how.

Notes

1. The Unexpected Legacy of Divorce – A 25 Year Landmark Study: Introduction, page xxii – xv. Authors Judith Wallerstein, Julia Lewis and Sandra Blakeslee – Hyperion Publishing, Copyright 2000

CHAPTER 1

The Forgotten Option

"I pray that your love will overflow more and more, and that you will keep on growing in knowledge and understanding. For I want you to understand what really matters . . . . ."

Paul
Philippians 1:9 - 10
New Living Translation

What Is The Forgotten Option?

I have had so many personal and public experiences regarding faithfulness in marriage and how it should be defined, that I see that the truth is a bit 'fuzzy' lately. In other words, as some have begun to operate from self-centeredness and their own opinions, the concept of marriage is becoming a bit crazy out here. For me, the natural outcome over all the confusion and hurt I see was to think about this essential relationship in life. Could it still be the very thing that people dream about? There is nothing wrong with dreaming about a successful and happy marriage – it is just noticeably hard for some to imagine this as they view the landscape of our day and the confusion of our age. But I have found that the hope of many is that marriage will be meaningful to their hearts and lives, and that the true white knight will come shining through. Hold that thought dear to your chest, for it is possible.

I've heard from many in Christian circles about all of the options that we have if your marriage is difficult, too hard or intolerable to you. Yet in my studies of our foundational truths I didn't see the 'many options' that these people talked about in Christianity, especially in the guidelines that Jesus gave for ending marriage. I just saw 'an option', one that was not commanded by Him but conceded as necessary to those who needed it. Within the book that carries this singular option also comes an overwhelming amount of additional information, which states that marriage and the family are very important to God and that we should remain faithful to this commitment for life. But I don't know that we see it this way anymore; we're focused on other things. May I be so bold to say that

3

He esteems marriage to a higher level than many of the things that we would pick and choose from. Like captains of our own ships, when the storms of life hit we seem to be throwing the most precious cargo over first; things that He would keep on board – storms or not.

The Apostle Paul, following up on Jesus' statements on marriage and divorce, uncovered a major point, in my opinion, on how to work out difficulties and stay in a marriage. The principle he talks about has also has been confirmed to me by the events I have witnessed, stories I have heard and marriages I've seen that have been changed for the good. The point I refer to is where Paul speaks to wives, asking them not separate from their husbands (see below). But if a woman did, she was to remain unmarried or else leave open the option of coming back into the marriage. The same holds true for a man.

'But for those who are married, I have a command that comes not from me, but from the Lord. A wife must not leave her husband. But if she does leave him, let her remain single or else be reconciled to him. And the husband must not leave his wife.'[1]

He famously says that this reference comes from God; meaning it wasn't something that he made up.

⌐

We know from Jesus' statements in the New Testament on marriage and divorce that women have left their original marriages over the span of history, just the same as men have. He speaks to this issue, as we shall see, in one of His talks on this subject. I personally don't know how divorce worked for women in all cultures over all time – I just know that it took place.

The word 'separate' that Paul uses here in this passage is followed by the statement that she is to 'remain unmarried'. From reviewing various translations I found that several versions left this word as 'separate', but other versions translated the same word as 'to depart' or to 'divorce'. Not only does the context of a woman remaining unmarried seem to confirm that to separate might have meant divorce, but Paul goes on in this sentence to give the same admonition to men also. He says, in the same way, ". . and a husband should not divorce his wife.'

This means several key things are here for us to consider.

One, marriage in God's plan of things is meant to stay intact. I have no doubts that Paul was speaking for God in this verse as he said because all the statements of Jesus confirm what Paul is saying. The family is too precious to dissolve for all the reasons some want to give today. The only 'out' He allowed, known to many, was over sexual unfaithfulness. The point here is people were not to be locked into marriages where someone obviously conveys that they want to be one with someone else. However, as we can see by the life of Hosea and others, dissolving the family was not commanded by God but only served as a necessary concession when needed. It might be a greater act of love to resolve such issues if possible, for some couples have worked their way back from unfaithfulness and in the process have saved their families and future generations as a result. They are regarded as examples of amazing, miraculous reconciliations in their own circles and I too honor these who have the ability to take love to this greater length and depth.

Secondly, Paul's directive to stay together is for a situation where a divorce or a permanent parting most likely had taken place, probably due to an issue thought unresolvable by the couple. As I read between the lines I see Paul understanding the difficulties that a couple might face, but also knowing that God commanded they stay together. But if Paul's statement here had any grounding in an adultery having taken place, he would have mentioned it and the statement would have gone a different direction.

So what are the ramifications of this then?

I think it shows that people get overwhelmed with life and think their marriage is the issue. Maybe they put rings on each other but lack 90% of the skills required to keep them on. It may also show that people get self-centered and can make hasty decisions that are not well thought out. In most cases the divorces I see seem to fall in these categories. Regardless of whether we've made the wrong decisions, lack the skills or life is too hectic, it appears to many that what's done is done and there is nothing more that can be un-done about it. They're divorced and it's over.

However, it appears that God looks at divorce differently than we do. It is interesting to me that most see divorce today as a permanent dissolution of the marriage, where Jesus and Paul did not. I see it as they do also. Regardless of a piece of paper coming from a courthouse, what Jesus emphasized and what Paul also confirms, is that divorce doesn't mean that a marriage is finished. If you leave a marriage for other than justifiable reasons, God would have you to stay single or else leave the door open for one or the other of you to come back into the original marriage. To leave a marriage and marry another, for any reason other than adultery, says you have broken the true marriage vows. Hear me on this or listen to God instead. We are to stay in the position we find ourselves in and wait for further orders. There is no clock ticking, nor a certain amount of time called out, no final curtain call to where you are now allowed to be free of the other party. Divorce, to me, is just the most severe argument a couple can have. But, if left alone by others and not subjected to poor counsel, a broken marriage can be eventually resolved and the couple brought back together again – to the betterment of us all – even if you and I don't know them.

Thirdly, if the word separation means divorce in Paul's example, maybe we have missed what true separation without divorce really means. When not meant as an end to a marriage, I believe we need to understand how effective it can be to give a marriage or a marriage partner 'time out' to think over the poor behaviors that they are manifesting. In days gone by it was said that a wife went 'to visit her mother' when a husband had acted poorly. That was a truth that came from the generation before mine where divorce was rare – maybe for reasons like this. When done properly and with good counsel, times apart can be necessary corrections to keep a ship on course. All this about separation without divorce needs to be understood however as being steps taken for the purpose of eventual reconciliation, not steps made to leave the marriage. This needs to be crystal clear, especially to the marriage partner being affected, before any subsequent actions are taken.

Fourth, we need to recognize that some cannot take the situation they are in but must leave – whether for a while or a longer period of time. What would seem workable to a marriage counselor or to others you know may be too much for the person involved. Other people cannot draw your lines for you. Mark Twain related how he saw his daughter befuddled to the point of tears over a simple situation regarding her doll, or something like this. In his compassion for her he understood that this wasn't an issue that brought him to tears, but in her world it did. In the same way, you alone must determine what is livable for your situation and what is not. I think the proper caution here, from Paul as well as from others, would be to make sure of several things:

A. Verify within yourself that the issue at hand is really an unlivable situation worth leaving for. Be aware that there are temptations out there. There are also people that would prey on your situation of being alone, if allowed to meddle in your affairs unchecked.

B. If you leave, determine that it is with the idea of bringing about reconciliation – not separation leading to divorce forever.

C. Balance all this with the concept that separations can be for an hour, an afternoon, a day, a week or longer – whatever it takes to begin to see the changes needed. They can be incremental and sequential steps going forward until more serious measures need to be ultimately reached – if necessary.

D. And finally, if the matter at hand *is an issue* for you, don't wait until things are out of control. Begin to set your guidelines as early as possible. Do whatever is necessary to not put yourself or your family in harm's way by allowing things to become dangerous or unsafe. Get help if needed. You can be just as faithful in a safe location farther away as you can be in your own home.

～

I have had the unfortunate experience of being separated for good from the one I loved, without any opportunity to resolve the issue, and not because of reasons of sexual unfaithfulness. Bear in mind that I was a problem. I was not a great guy to be with or be around and I had changes to make. But I still wanted to be loved like anyone would and also save our family unit that I loved as well.

It was during this time in my life, while in a doctor's office, I heard of a marriage situation similar to mine but with way different results. Because things had been handled differently by one of the marriage partners, the other partner, the family and the marriage had been restored. I will relate this story in the pages ahead, but from this experience I began to see how important separation can be to resolve unresolvable issues, when done correctly. I had seen personally how time apart had been necessary for me. As hard headed as I was, to have a line drawn in the sand saying 'no more' was what it took for me to get my eyes opened up as they should have been all along. To be separated from my family, as bad as it was, gave me an opportunity to think about what I had done and who I had been. It was helpful to me to have had the pain of going through this situation, that was forced upon me, as a catalyst for my change. During this time alone I also saw hope. I saw evidence of the fact that I truly wanted to be a better man by the changes I made. I also saw the values that I was supposed to have upheld all along starting to take root within me.

Sadly, the option to return to the marriage was not extended; no such olive branch ever arrived – even to this day. Another marriage took place and the door was shut in my face forever. My hope is that some sort of peace between us will come. Though we can't turn back the pages of our lives, at least we could represent - going forward - true forgiveness, reconciliation and friendship among ourselves as the parents to our kids. This is one of my greatest dreams and desires.

In the meantime I have seen the fallout from these issues that could have been resolved take hold of my family and our extended community - in ways that haven't been good. I have seen what could have been avoided if reconciliation had been offered. Many others like me had no real intention of ultimately wanting to destroy our marriages and our families; and even though in our immaturity we said and did hateful things, we just needed to be taught a tough lesson. Being set apart from your family is a very telling thing. To some it means nothing and they go on their way, thus confirming their spouse's fears that this person they married didn't really care about them at all. This is sad to me personally. But in many other cases, times like this are a necessary wake-up call that can bring about the redemption of a person, a marriage and a family - if done right. I am an advocate for times apart, when needed, but I am not an advocate for divorce. I realize without an ability to draw boundaries, when some reach their limits and think they have no other option, that often times lines are drawn permanently that could have been resolved in other lesser ways.

Thus, the importance of translating 'separation' in Paul's writing into the proper concept of a divorce became a very important thing for me to look at. And from what I have seen and experienced, it could be as equally important to others like you as well.

⌒

The Forgotten Option then is about making the right decisions in God's way.

It certainly is about marriage faithfulness – make no mistake of this. I would be the wrong person to see if you are considering leaving your marriage. Any spouse who undermines their marriage, short or long term, is undermining their own best interests. In addition this book is about the 'options' you have at your disposal to stay *within your marriage* successfully.

But it is ultimately about how proper moments of separation, if used carefully and with good counsel, may not only redeem the issues that you see dissolving your marriage but redeem the person you married also. So many see just two options – marriage or divorce – when there is another short-term solution that can be used.

Often couples come from homes where faithfulness, forgiveness and marriage relationships were not modeled correctly. They could use help to see what marriage can look like for them and some allowance to work through the issues they inherited through the example of a poor home life. They need to know how marriage can work when the right skills are put into place. Actions like the ones I will mention better define what love should truly look like to me, than everyone just leaving their relationship for good.

If what I've said interests you, I hope you'll join me.

Notes

1. On marriage and divorce - Paul: The New Testament - 1 Corinthians, chapter 7:10 [New Living Translation - NLT]

Who This Book Is For

This is a book on marriage, being married and how to ultimately stay married.

I think with the events of today there are many who wonder if they can make it in a marriage. It is my premise that you can. Just know a little bit about yourself, be patient enough to choose your partner carefully and you're going to be over 90% there. And if you feel you haven't done any of the above, don't jump ship – there is hope. It is my second premise that there may be places where people need growth, maybe even to be apart for a season in difficult to extreme situations, but having you remaining in or heading back to your marriage is the goal. It is my reason for writing this – with the hope that I can help in a small way to make this happen for you.

This book is chiefly aimed at first marriages and how to have your best chance of succeeding in them. I am not being segregated in my feelings toward people that find themselves in other marriages; I just firmly believe that the first marriage is where your greatest blessing will be. I say this word 'blessing' in a personal sense first of all, directed just towards you. But I also mean this in a larger sense, for there are those around you too that depend on your marriage and your example to be an encouragement to them. I just have seen that the first marriage is where God can do the most good for you, making necessary changes in you and in those that surround you if we'll just stick it out. No man or woman is an island, and no marriage exists alone. Many lives will be affected by the decisions you both make. But know that you deserve His best blessings, whether you believe in this or not.

And possibly - through you and the decisions you can make - your family, extended family, your community and future generations can experience these blessings too.

With that said, there are several categories we may find ourselves in.

1. **You're single**, and with all you see you're wondering if you can make it in a marriage. I'm here to tell you that you can – you just need to think things out and resolve some issues ahead of time.

2. **You are among those who are married, whether things are good or bad.** Ideally, I think you ought to have your marriage goals and focus set out before you prior to setting sail, with the plan of both of you reaching dry land on the other side. If that hasn't happened yet it can happen now. In addition, like the way a lifejacket or a small dingy is found onboard a cruise ship, you ought to have your own avenues of rescue prepared ahead of time if you run into troubles. The real tragedy of the Titanic is not that the ship went down, but that so few lives were saved. The absence of a proper number of lifeboats became a thing of the past after that tragic voyage.

    In the same way our goal here is to save couples, not letting them drown or die, for in saving a marriage we hope to save precious individuals as well. So have an emergency plan or several laid out; have your lifeboats set-up and your crew of faithful friends that will be there to encourage you towards the right shore. You ought to know just what you would do and where you would go in case things got bad for you or the ones that you love. No one hopes it never gets to that point – but this is just in case.

3. **You're among those who are not together - but still married to each other.** The spot you are in seems like

'no man's land'. It feels like you are not in a relationship but you are not out of one either – and you probably want to end this confusion. Your former friends may be divided in their allegiance, and so you may find yourself alone without a full support team as well. Given all this, you may think that this spot you are in is a place to be avoided; that you need to move out of this transitionary location as soon as possible into another relationship – but I caution 'NO!' The last image of your marriage may appear to be a nightmare and a future destination with someone else may beckon like an advertisement for a brand new car or a tropical vacation spot. You may want to be rescued by a handsome prince from the toad of before, but I assure you that you are in the right spot to remain as you are – at least for now. Take a breath, settle down, make yourself safe, and keep yourself single. Then at least hear God out and understand what He would want for your life.

4. **You are among those who are divorced but both parties haven't remarried anyone else yet.** I would say to you that there is yet hope. I am surprised at how 'final' some people regard divorce to be – but it's not. I've seen divorces resolved and marriages revived too many times. Truly, there has most likely been some minor or major damage done, and it is the most serious fight or argument you can ever pick with a spouse – but there is still hope. So much is at stake. You are both still alive, you can both speak, see and hear – and I find that very encouraging at the least. What I am saying therefore is there is still room to communicate. Your marriage isn't terminal until one or both of you are gone from this earth – or until one of you marries another. Like Bob, a friend of mine, said, "You don't lose money until you sell" – so don't sell - hold on.

This situation incidentally is what makes divorce so painful; the other person is alive and at least one [or both] of you longs for reconciliation. In every divorce situation there is usually one who wanted out, but almost always there is another who wanted them to stay. It just takes one, however, to be hard-hearted and the other has to live with the outcome. Not only will there be the pain of a legal breaking up of the marriage relationship, but the additional hurt of possibly having to watch as another marriage takes your place. We want both of you to take a break if need be, but not break up for good.

5. **Lastly, you may have had past marriage issues but now you have gotten re-married to someone else**. This book may still be helpful to you. If you have made the second most important decision in life for a second time, you are now to be committed to your new life and your new partner. I don't know what problems you may have brought into this new relationship, but my highest desire for you is that you will be faithful to your new marriage. Maybe it is too bold and presumptuous to say that if I had written this earlier, or if you had gotten better counsel, you might have made a different decision. I don't know that for sure, but that door is forever closed. Now, keeping your second marriage intact should be your reasonable goal. However, it may take the same amount of soul searching and honesty you should have had the first time around to make this marriage work.

⟿

Know that I have tried to write this book, in part, for those who have a non-religious viewpoint. This is because I don't want to ostracize anyone – truly. I don't think that I succeeded very well in this effort to the extent that I would have liked, but it was a goal of mine just the same. All I can say in a non-religious way is the first marriage has the best chance of providing the joy, happiness and success that you truly want and need. It is where your character can be developed and finally find its rest. It's where others around you can be blessed and encouraged because of the decisions you've made along the way. I believe this to be true, God or not. How you get there without the directions God provides is up to you to figure out however.

To those who are Christians as I am, I am going to present the opportunity for us to be authentic. The world wants to see it. We may have the key that unlocks heaven's door through Jesus's work on the cross, but our lives may still be discouraging to others - even harmful – because of the way we live. I want you to have another key that God has provided. Like the first, this key has eternal ramifications too, but this key is mainly for this life and this time of ours on earth. God wants to unlock incredible changes in your life through your being able to understand His Word [its guidance] and His will for you. An open ear and hopefully obedience to what you hear is all that is required from you.

A verse that speaks of what I am saying here goes like this,

'Now all glory to God, who is able, through His mighty power at work within us, to accomplish infinitely more than we might ask or think. Glory to Him in the church and in Christ Jesus through all generations, for ever and ever! Amen.'[1]

We all want miraculous things to happen all *around* us. Maybe we want Him to bring whales close to shore so we see or swim with them. Maybe we want Him to make us rich, save our marriages with the snap of His fingers, or create happiness for us by a wave of His hand. These are externals - but the real miracles He wants to see in this world are not external; they are *internal, within us*. These changes He wants for us are what He calls immeasurably, exceedingly and abundantly more that we could ask or hope for – all done by His power that can be at work within any of us. It is our choice to make.

Can you imagine how happy you would be to see this prayer answered in your own life? To see changes that you've longed for in the areas of love, your attitude, your work ethic and the patience you wish you had. To see personal goals, financial goals and desires you have longed for in your future finally happen. Imagine seeing changes within you that would ensure your ability to adequately love others. Imagine seeing accomplishments coming out of your life that ultimately are for the benefit others, finally tapping into what God has wanted for you to be all along. This would be the highest form of a miracle that we could ask for, if it happened in your life or mine.

Changes within us, to God's good standards, are what make all other things possible. The world around us is waiting to see our changes. There would be less crime, divorce, arguments, adultery, running away from our responsibilities, drug use, and more of the same – if we all had a proper change of heart and mind.

In one section of the Bible it says,

'Since they thought it foolish to acknowledge God, He abandoned them to their foolish thinking and let them do things that should never be done. Their lives became full of every kind of wickedness, sin, greed, murder, quarreling, deception, malicious behavior, and gossip. They are backstabbers, haters of God, insolent, proud and boastful. They invent new ways of sinning, and they disobey their parents. They refuse to understand, break their promises, are heartless, and have no mercy.'[2]

We don't have to go this way. A proper change of heart and mind within us is what the God of the Bible is all about.

⤿

This is the first book I've ever written to completion, and finally published.

When asked by others as to what I was writing, I have never gotten a negative response when I explained what I am going to address with you here. This has been a motivator to me, beyond the convictions I already had, to keep on going.

My first motivation to write, in the beginning, was because of the hurt and painful fallout I saw over divorce and failed marriages all around me. My second motivation was due to the bad advice I believe that is being given on how to solve the problems that are found in difficult marriage situations.

Many people, professionals and pastors too, look at marriage in only 2 ways.

A. You're either married and successful at it (or maybe you're just holding on)
B. You're having major problems and you're on your way to a divorce.

So the message is – is it door 'A' or door 'B'? When we have problems do we file to the right side or file to the left? There is no mention of an in between place where multiple options exist that is recognized as being important or valid. And though this two point plan has led to poor theology, bad advice, shattered lives and characters being destroyed in our culture – we continue to march on. Some even attempt to validate their position.

But there still are the human remnants of these discouraging situations before us in society and also in the churches that we inhabit, that we have to look on week, after week, after week. Without a different plan being advocated, we are silently endorsing ridiculous behaviors in society and in Christianity, that only continue to propagate the misfortunes we find in our midst. I may sound like I have a bias, but it's not just Christian marriages that I'm worried about. All marriages are important to me. I want to direct my energies accordingly in as many directions as I can.

Notes

1. Not externals, but what He can do in us: Ephesians, chapter 3:20-21 [New Living Translation – NLT]
2. A proper change of heart and mind being what's needed: Romans, chapter 1:28 – 31 [NLT]

CHAPTER **2**

About Men and Women

Giving Eve to Adam

Giving Eve to Adam

After God created Adam, and all the details regarding the names of the animals, sorting out the plant life and finalizing the arrangements for taking care of the garden were worked out, Adam showed up one day to talk with God.

He said, "I see that all the animals - the hippos, lions and all other living things of the ground, the sea and the air - have their mates, but I don't. I am not complaining – the Garden of Eden is lovely and I am taken back with all You've made and the stars that shine up above, but I get lonely at night just looking at them alone. Is there anyone for me?"

God said, "Adam, I had something already in mind – I was just waiting for you to ask."

Adam smiled. A sigh of relief came from his lips and joy filled his heart.

"Just go back and lie down for the evening," God said, "and I will take care of it."

Do you know this part of the story – possibly from your childhood days?

Adam lay down and God took a bone that evening from Adams body while he was in a deep sleep. The bone was not from his feet to be under him, nor from his head to be over him, but from near his heart to be dear to him and from his body to be one with him. From this He made Eve. As Adam stood before God and looked at what He created, he thought she was so lovely. He was amazed at how she was like him, but in a different way. Her shoulders were sculptured like a beautiful hill, her hair was like a waterfall coming down a tall mountain side, her voice was like the music of a brook and her eyes were the fairest sunset he had ever seen. She was sweet, she had curves that were beautiful to look at, and Eve seemed to contain a quality that he would later understand as being 'feminine'. His heart was filled beyond measure and he knew he would never have to ask God for anything more.

The Lord smiled as they walked away together, hand in hand, and He went back to His work.

A few months later Adam came back to see the Lord.

"God, this woman you made me seemed to be a good idea in the beginning, but there have been problems of late. My appearance that she thought was fine at first is now not good enough. She picks at my hair and wants me to stand up straighter. And the bed of grass I slept on in the grove beneath the stars is now too hard and firm for her; she wants to lie on a bed of feathers, much like a birds nest. Using the forest for my needs was OK with me personally, but now she wants something 'private'. She wants to talk into the night when I'm tired and she asks dumb questions like, "Adam, do you like my hair?"

Adam paused and looked at God through disappointed eyes. "Is there any chance we could 'undo' this thing you call a woman?"

"Sure Adam," God replied, "just leave it to Me." And God took Eve away.

It was only a matter of weeks and God heard a voice behind Him, like someone clearing their throat, to get His attention. He turned and saw Adam.

"God," Adam said haltingly, "it's about Eve. I think I made a mistake. Everything I said before was true, but there were also the good things that I left out. She was warm to sleep with and to hear her even breath at night was comforting to me. She did pick at me sometimes, but there were so many other times that we laughed together with such joy in our hearts. The stars seemed to have a different tint with her around and I loved hearing her sing in the distance, because I knew she was around me."

Adam looked down at the ground for a moment, in a kind of gesture of shame, and then eventually looked up to speak. "I'm sorry God, is there any chance I could get her back?"

God smiled and said, "Sure Adam." And He gave Eve back to Adam.

It was only a few days this time and God heard the same muffled cough behind Him as before. He turned to see Adam.

"God," Adam said, "Things haven't changed as I thought they would. It seems that it's all started up again, just where it left off. I think I'm sure this time – can You take her back again?"

God stopped for a moment and looked knowingly at Adam. He said, "Son, I think you're going to find that you can't live with her and you can't live without her."

And with that, God just turned around and went back to His work.

⌒

This is just a fictional story, but if I say nothing else of value I hope you will understand the truth it gives.

The message is that love between any two people, as real as it is, will be mixed with a host of difficulties. You may initially lack a lot of the necessary skill sets – but you can learn them over time and gain the skills you need. There are times you will feel great about being together and times you will wonder what you did by marrying this other person. Fear and uncertainty, telling you that you should have done life differently, will dog your steps. There may be seasons where you will mistakenly inter-mingle your own personal issues with your marriage. Things can come into harm your relationship together, especially when you may be weary or fearful. You may be dealing with health, emotional, family or vocational problems. It doesn't mean your marriage is bad, it just means that you need separate help in other areas of your life.

Love will often be the most painful thing that you will ever feel. But amazingly, and I think few recognize this; love has a life of its own and will never die. That means love will bless you in the long run if you stay, but will hurt forever if you turn your back and walk away from it. 'Stick with it' is my message - for an amazing thing has taken place when you mix two lives together. You undoubtedly will have to look up often for encouragement and strength, but you can make it. God won't turn His back on you.

If you can acknowledge that you have often felt the same way Adam does [Eve too, but we didn't tell her side of the story], then you are human and not alone. This is the life that we live, with its ups and downs. Realizing we have these times, though they are scary and challenging, is the perfect place for us to start.

So I want to look at us, men and women, then dating and love next; for these issues are before marriage and they are the true beginnings of how two lives become one.

Women

"Whether women are better than men I cannot say . . . .
but I can say they are certainly no worse."
Golda Meir / former Prime Minister of Israel

Some Thoughts on Women

Peter Marshall, the Scottish born American preacher, who was pastor of the New York Avenue Presbyterian Church in Washington D.C., and Chaplin of the U.S. Senate, wrote about a man in the hills who kept the water in his town safe to drink. Quietly moving about above the town, he removed the silt, leaves, mud and mold to keep pure water flowing down the mountain to the people living below. In the story Marshall likens the role of women to this man above in the hills, calling for their help to keep society clean and on track. The sermon, called 'The Keeper of the Springs', I consider a must for you go over sometime and hope you'll seek it out to read it in its entirety.

It is one of my favorite reflections on women. I like the way it speaks of the gentleness and wonder that is a woman – of purity and the finer things that she is made of and capable of.

From my own experience, I think of women like the height Mount Everest or the floor of Death Valley, and all points in between – depending on the woman and the circumstances. I have seen women in their lofty moments of dignity and achievement, where they shine like the stars and seem to visit the heavens above. And sadly, I have also seen the incredible lows they can stoop to; dishonoring and undermining, in my opinion, the very concept of what a woman was designed to be.

I believe that they all are very gifted and smart – dwarfing men often in their various abilities - except generally in the physical realm. I don't want to incite anyone to heresy, but given this, is it wrong to wonder if God at least considered creating woman first and then making man second? She was already talented, pretty and highly capable - above a man in many ways – why not just let her run the whole show? It's just theorization, but if a shred of it were true, God obviously went another direction. I believe He had a legitimate reason for making woman second.

First, to be superior in so many ways and to have her also take the lead would have been too much for her character. In fact, it would have been too much for anyone's character. A step like this would have most likely opened up too much of a chance for ages of selfishness to come thereafter. It would be too hard for anyone in her situation, with all this going for them, to not have their ego, attitude and character get out of balance. Secondly, the whole thing would have been unfair to men. With all the giftedness that women possess, she would have looked down on man and left him in the dust. God would let her keep her giftedness, but He would need to balance things out a little better instead.

God, in fact, did make her second. It was not because she wasn't equal to men, no, she was far more than that – but He made her second to save her in the long run and to temper her giftedness a bit. He gave her a far greater task, one to which she was equal to and made for. He would ask her to volunteer for a support role. He wanted her to take all of her giftedness and develop those who needed her insight – the men, children, families and communities of this world. She is to take her talents and support a man to help him become a better man, attaining heights he hadn't thought were possible on his own. Such a man who saw her as she really is wouldn't think of belittling her. God, I think, was counting on men to see this. A right thinking man would just hope that she would love him enough to wait at each step for him to catch up.

In the annals of history, it is written that Solomon asked God to give him wisdom for a purpose. He was young and inexperienced and needed help – so he asked for the ability to govern the Nation of Israel wisely and it was done for him by God. A lot of his failures from that point on were all due to using his wisdom selfishly; turning it toward his *own* pleasures and away from its intended purpose of leading Israel wisely. He was to use it for the betterment of the people of his nation.

In like fashion, I think when women free themselves from guiding, helping and lifting others up, but seek only to be first again and put everything else below them, they are out of balance. They are not where God intended them to be when they are only out for themselves; they weren't designed for it. Selfishness, like the depths of Death Valley, is a direction that God feared women *could* take but never intended for them to go. It's not the servanthood they are called to, but a dominance they are capable of that leads to increasing darkness for all involved. It is their talents missing the mark and egos gone rampant. It's not being compassionate to men, children or the family unit, but regarding all these to some degree with disdain. It is looking upon her God given duties as impositions that hold her down, like a kite tied to a string. It is a hardness of heart toward the task God gave them that most assuredly doesn't come easily for women - all recognize this - but none the less is the work that they were gifted to do.

This type of misdirection, prevalent among some women today, is the only way I can understand the confusion of what I see at times in certain circles.

I know that women in general, in past decades, were more economically bound and dependent on their husbands than they are today. If life was difficult for them there wasn't much they could do about it. Today, with women in the market place often making great incomes and being very successful, theirs is now the challenge of not becoming too independent and too self-consumed with themselves or their careers.

I would ask women to think of your husband and your children as a corporation that needs to be run successfully. You are what I would call 'the silent CEO' and the only one who can make that corporation become organized enough to thrive during normal and difficult times. It is up to you to help if the corporation is ultimately going to become successful or not. Are you going to trade being in charge of your own company for a job that is someone else's dream? Are you going to be one of many hourly employees wandering about instead of managing your own firm? This doesn't make sense to me. It doesn't mean that you can't be a successful professional, but don't lose sight of the family unit. Your family corporation is so much more profitable and valuable than your day job.

I went to a fly-in, years ago, where some vintage WWII aircraft were going to be displayed. I will never forget seeing a B-17 bomber there for the first time in my life. Knowing its overall effect on the war by running bombs out of England into the heart of the German war machine, I had always thought that it was a large plane. I was surprised however to see how small, by today's standards, it really was. As I walked through its cramped interior I thought of how heroic it was for the men who comprised its crews to go on these missions, knowing that many of them would not come back alive. Speaking with one of the men who was a part of the group that flew the B-17 in to the event, I asked him what his most memorable experience was in being associated with this plane. Without hesitation he told me that when they had flown into Seattle he saw a woman come up to the side of the aircraft's fuselage and started counting spots on the skin as she walked outward towards the wing tip. She got about halfway out, stopped, and started to cry. A bit dumbfounded, this gentleman I was speaking with approached her and asked if she was OK. Through tears she said, "These are my rivets."

She had worked in production plant in Seattle during the war and this location on the aircraft wing had been her assigned spot to drive rivets. I like my job but I don't cry when I see some of the things I've been a part of; but this was more important. These were different times and her task was critical. Like a mother hen, she probably wondered over the years how many of her 'rivets', carrying those boys to the sky, were going to come back. On this day she was relieved to see another one of her rows - the fruit of her hard work. When you think of your task as a woman, I hope you will see that it is even more important than hers; that you will look into the future by faith and wonder how your influence in your family will make a difference, and how many you will 'bring home' as well.

⤳

There are women who work regular jobs and help to provide a portion of the budget for their family income, but they need help to run the family business. They often don't get the help they need. Is it too much for them to work, help their husbands, devote time to the care of the kids and run the household also? Yes, I think it is. When they are stressed out, with all these expectations, duties and pressures upon them, it's no wonder that some of them make poor choices about the life they want to have. They need the husband they have to care for them and jump in to help. Sure there are stresses in today's world, but it is better that 2 people share them together than just one alone.

There are also natural feelings from childhood that affect women too.

Ever since they were little girls, most women had visions of a home like a castle with obedient children and a husband who was like Sir Lancelot. That kind of childhood dream brings high expectations into adulthood.

Most of us guys didn't have dreams of being Sir Lancelot (I guess we should have) – we just played soldiers. We brandished twigs that were imaginary swords and probably more resembled Huck Finn, floating idly down the river on a raft with a straw of grass coming out of our mouths. More often than not, we were more the free and easy kind of boy than one who was focused on being a knight in shining armor. Most of us guys, from early childhood into later adult years, didn't get the memo on how girls thought we should be. Add to that the aspect of not being raised in a home where dad and mom stayed together. We might not have had the advantage of seeing how it should be done – the proper interplay that should take place between a husband and a wife.

So it would be easy for disillusionment to set in when the husband turns out to be an average guy – or maybe less than average - and even has a bit of an attitude to boot. And if he's just a basic guy and not Superman, at some point, a general hopelessness about her husband and his capabilities can take place. She just gets afraid of the future she will have with her man. If she feels that things are too hard for her or too disappointing, and she just can't take it anymore, the abandon ship alarm may begin to ring in her head. Some women face their fears and their tasks; others jump overboard and are gone.

Fear for a woman may appear to be real, or in fact is real. There possibly and truly are difficult things ahead that she might have to deal with and to face. Know that I never advocate that a woman or her children should ever be in a place of real or potential danger.

One of the more famous personalities of the New Testament times, Peter the Apostle, talked about how women fear and what the outcome could be.

'Don't be concerned about the outward beauty of fancy hairstyles, expensive jewelry or beautiful clothes. You should clothe yourselves instead with the beauty that comes from within, the unfading beauty of a gentle and quiet spirit, which is so precious to God. This is how the holy women of old made themselves beautiful. **They trusted God** and accepted the authority of their husbands. For instance, Sarah obeyed her husband, Abraham, and called him her master. **You are her daughters when you do what is right without fear of what your husbands might do.**'[1]

You would have to know about Sarah's circumstances, and what she had to deal with, to understand the depth of what Peter is saying. That might be the subject of another book.

Just know that fear, protection, and security are a large part of what stresses women out. It is difficult for them to deal with life without these things. It's understandable that women want security; what I think they miss is that men want it too, and that for all of us it is a rare, precious commodity.

'Then said Mr. Contrite to them, "Pray, how fareth it with you in your pilgrimage? How stands the country affected towards you?"

Honesty: "It happens to us as it happeneth to wayfaring men – sometimes our way is clean, sometimes foul, sometimes up-hill, sometimes down-hill; we are seldom at a certainty; the wind is not always on our backs, nor is every one a friend that we meet with in the way. We have met with some notable rubs already, and what are yet behind we know not, but for the most part we find it true, that has been talked of, of old, 'A good man must suffer trouble.'"[2]

It's how we go about finding security, and the decisions we make to apprehend it, that is critical to our souls.

⤿

There is one more matter directed at women that is especially concerning to me.

There is an attitude that is more and more prevalent in some feminine circles that it is *all about women*. It's to the point that 'me too' is now turning into 'me first' or 'me only'. There are a growing number who advocate that their body is their own and that what they do with their lives is their decision *solely* – even though it is not. Common sense and logic would tell you that there are others involved. I see any movement - propagating the concept that women have the right to pursue what they want, without any regard for the affect it has on others; be it a spouse, their family, those close to them or those far away – as having already become a dangerous course.

It is concerning for anyone, male or female, to think or act just in terms of what alone makes *them* happy. The cause and effect upon the circumstances around them need to be weighed in as well. Looking at human behavior, one only needs to view history to see how terrible things can get when propagators of heinous deeds were found to only be focused on themselves. It is a perilous place and a slippery slope for anyone of us to be in when we have this mind set.

It's interesting to me that the best-selling book of all time mentions that the last days of human history will bring terrible times. We all sense that this could be true. At the same time, and far more confusing, it says that in those final days there will be a great movement of love. These two things don't make sense to me - something sounds wrong. Love and the most terrible time in history - how could this be?

The movement of love it speaks of is not a love for others however, but is a self-love only. It is not the kind of self-love you should have for good self-esteem either – it goes beyond this. It is an all-consuming, self-focused view of life that tries to make the world spin around my wishes and desires. It is a love for oneself that will put not just their 'needs', but their wants and desires also, above all others and all other things. It will not be a natural type of love that makes someone stop their car for a person stranded on the side of the road, it is a self-love where I drive by because I have far more important things to do than help you. It may or may not be the end of world yet, but we're seeing glimpses of this today on a smaller scale – and what we are seeing appears to be growing more and more potentially destructive.

I think you can see the 'me first' attitude affecting marriage as well. It is almost an unimaginable statistic that exists today, but of the divorces in the United States a staggering 80% of them are initiated by women. If this data were turned around and it was men that I was speaking about, I would be ashamed for those of my own gender and alarmed at the same time. I would be wondering if men in general had lost their minds. It would be hard for me to be linked to this statistical data and find it easy to hold my head up too high as a man. Should I feel differently about this because it is about women instead?

A final note.

When I used to go to the barber near where I lived in Washington, one of the ladies in the shop was especially good at cutting my hair. I always selected her if she was in. She was Vietnamese and a first generation immigrant to the United States. In our talks together while I was in her chair we spoke many times about her kids and on the subject of family and marriage. She described the discipline she was installing into her children – that of education, being respectful to family members, to school teachers, and teaching them to save their money. When we talked about marriage and the divorce rates that exist in the United States, she offered her perspective.

"Women in the US are spoiled," she said. "It seems like they want their own way. They are just thinking of themselves and have little regard for their families." She wasn't angry or condescending, but spoke in matter-of-fact tones – stating her concerns. "In our culture," she said, "men are mostly dominant, it's true, and there are some women who don't have good marriages." She wasn't speaking of a dangerous situation, but of a less than ideal husband. "However, the women from my country will put up with a bad marriage, if necessary, rather than inflict suffering and hurt upon our own children." It was an amazing thing to hear.

Her perspective was challenging and noble to me, not because I like any man to be unmindful of his wife or dominant, but because she saw the bigger picture which included her kids and extended family members too. I have not forgotten that moment, or what she said.

It is for reasons like hers, that I am drawn to ask for a higher standard for all of us. Throughout this book I will contend over and over again that the original marriage has the best chance for the overall success of all involved. Even with all the potential problems, the first marriage is better than the other 'solutions' that are being freely offered today. I hope that women, and men too, will rise to the challenge of guarding their character by making better decisions – and to the best of their abilities put their families first.

Notes

1. On a woman's fear: 1 Peter, chapter 3:1 – 6 [NLT]
2. Pilgrim's Progress / John Bunyan

Men

"You have to be a man before you can be a gentleman."

John Wayne

Some Thoughts on Men

There is a story that goes something like this.

'After God created everything He made Eve. It wasn't too long after this that Adam came to him one day.

"It's amazing Lord; You've created radiant sunrises and sunsets, glorious waterfalls, beautiful plants, stunning animals of every kind that fill the seas, roam the earth and inhabit the skies, and majestic mountain scenery as well – but nothing is as beautiful or as wonderful to me as Eve. She moves my heart like nothing else you've created when I see her. Why did you make her so?"

"It was so you would love her," God said.

Adam had more on his mind. "After You made the animals I noticed that there were furs that were very pleasant to pet and run my hands over, flowers that were gentle to the touch and grasses that were thick and soft to lay on. But Lord, to touch her is amazing – unlike anything else. To feel her skin and to hold her close takes my breath away. Why did you make her so?"

"It was so you would love her," God said.

"One last thing Father," Adam said. "She seems to pester me at times. She pokes at me when I'm not sitting up straight and pouts when I'm not paying attention to her every moment. The whole thing seems so senseless. Why did you make her with the capacity to have these moments where she's so witless and silly?"

"It was so she could love you," God said. And with that He turned back to His work.'[1]

This is just a story and it doesn't mean that women are witless and silly; God says here fictionally that men are the ones in trouble.

41

God's miracle is that He changes women somehow to allow them to love us as men. If anything, this illustrates instead that men have their long moments of mental density - and that we really need some help.

꩜

Men know, usually, that they need help but we don't know to ask for it. We are either too proud or too afraid to reveal ourselves and our needs. We wonder if we're a man because we have to ask for help. But we need honest input from those who love us to face our responsibilities correctly, whether we want to hear it or not. In terms of advice, things go down easier when they're sweet, but just the same . . . . we need to get the message.

However, we usually don't see women in the right light that is necessary for our changes to take place.

When Jesus wrote in the dirt, a long time ago[2], He was addressing a host of men that were surrounding a woman. They had gone to find her for the sole purpose of shoving her in front of Him – the great teacher that He was – to get Him to capitulate on all this talk of love and mercy that He spoke of. She was of no consequence to them really – just a pawn to accomplish their purposes. I don't even know that they regarded her as a human being, to be honest.

So, when confronted with this whole situation, Jesus stooped down and spelled out words that we can only guess at today. The sands of time have erased His markings, which is just as well, for they were personal and specifically directed toward each one of the men before Him. And of the words he wrote, we know by the reaction He got that whatever He drew in the sand was pointed and convicting. It might have been names of other women that these men knew. It may have been dates, events and places that they thought were hidden behind the curtains of time, but now were in full view and exposed to those standing by. It was by this means He spelled out their hypocrisy. I believe He directed their actions and the contents of their personal lives back towards them in similar fashion to the way they directed theirs to this woman. It was another of many evidences to His deity; for having never met them personally or ever spent time with them physically, He knew all about their deeds and the secrets of their personal lives. It's the same today with each of us – regardless if we believe it or not.

There is no doubt that her story was not a pretty one and that she had been living a lifestyle of some degradation. She had been caught in promiscuity, and they knew who she was with and where to find her. So why didn't they bring the man that she was also with? They were looking down on her situation alone though, until He stooped to list, one by one and very specifically, what they had also done. Instead of continuing on their course of judgement and her punishment, they just turned and left, one by one, until there was no one left around her anymore. These men couldn't face the music themselves that they were playing just moments ago.

It seems occasionally that times haven't changed much.

From my vantage point, I feel that when the anti-abortion media goes after the perpetrators of abortion, it is usually only women that are mentioned. They seemingly are held accountable for the whole mess. But where are the men who fathered these children, who left their own offspring to face brutal circumstances and possible death by deserting their responsibilities? Should we follow the example of Jesus by stooping to write in the dirt, asking loudly and nationally, "Where are the men?" Remember that a child will always be a blessing to a couple who wants to be together and have a family. But it is most likely overwhelming to a woman, in that moment, when she is left alone to deal with this major responsibility without the other person around. It will be hard for her to come out of it making a proper decision. Fear can grip someone, anyone, to the point where they don't think rationally.

These women who are alone are susceptible to a host of voices, some of them good and some of them bad.

There are other situations like this that exist today that could all change in a moment, in the blink of an eye. If there are men who will rise to the occasion and take their responsibility, I don't think there would be as many children affected in the multitude of ways that we see now. This issue would be a minimal one. But if a man regards his relationship with a woman as a one night stand and an inconvenience; if he wants to call the whole thing off so he can go back to his old life, then nothing turns out as it should. Unfortunately there are women who come back to these men and who continue to go down the same paths with them – over and over again.

We can all be better men if we will just try. We should stand in the gap for ourselves to begin with, and then as men also stand in the gap for those we love. There are many lives that depend on us. We need to accept our responsibilities.

Contrary to popular opinion though, we're not made of steel. We need some help to be who we should be.

〜

I think men need to appreciate what they have in a wife and a woman.

Few men I've met have the wisdom to regard their wives in the correct way, to understand how much she can shape their lives in a positive direction if he will but properly seek out her counsel. Understanding a woman's attributes and abilities makes the concept of 'lording' ourselves over our wives a bit ridiculous. Instead, we should realize she was allowed to be a part of our lives for a reason, one of which might be to help us reach higher levels. Therefore, we should treat her thoughts with respect, contemplation and honor. It should make sense that this means we should spend more time with them than less, to gather their insights. I have been alone for a long time but I hope to have a special woman like this in my life someday, that I can trust and that she would feel the same way about me.

It is interesting to me that in the book of Proverbs it speaks of the virtuous woman – giving her a whole chapter. In case you're wondering, it may be sobering to know that there is no similar complete chapter devoted to men in Proverbs; hers is unique. As the book of Proverbs speaks of her, she has so many amazing attributes that it seems hard to believe that one person could have all this going for them.

It says in part,

> 'She finds wool and flax and busily spins it. She is like a merchant's ship, bringing food from afar. She gets up before dawn to prepare breakfast for her household and plan the day's work for her servant girls. She goes to inspect a field and buys it: with her earnings she plants a vineyard. She is energetic and strong, a hard worker. She makes sure her dealings are profitable; her lamp burns late into the night. She extends a helping hand to the poor and opens her arms to the needy. She has no fear of winter for her household, for everyone has warm clothes.'[3]

I particularly like how it speaks of her gathering her food from afar. She just doesn't go to the market and grab whatever's on the shelf. She cares about what she prepares, even if she has to go to great lengths to do it. To me it says that she wants her family and herself to eat healthy, balanced and nutritious meals, as much as possible.

And so on and on it wonderfully goes as it describes her.

But I have noticed something equally amazing in this passage. It says,

> **'Her husband is well known at the city gates, where he sits with the other civic leaders**. Her children stand

and bless her. Her husband praises her: "There are many virtuous and capable women in the world, but you surpass them all!"'[4]

Was he a self-made man before she arrived? We can assume that a smart woman would at least pick a man with potential. In a family close to me, the wife singled out her future husband when he was pretty rough around the edges. She would have passed by, but it took a Voice from above to say, "There is something here." Her choice of a man would not be who he is today without her. In like fashion, did the Proverbs man have his gifts already in motion, or was he brought to 'being' so to speak by her influence as well? The truth is at least one of these factors, probably both, were in operation at the time. For in this passage the man who ended up successful gave earned praise to his wife for her influence in his life.

I know of a woman who lost her first husband in death early on in their married life together. When he was alive he recognized her influence in his life as his partner and equal. All this had been years ago when the equal praise he gave her might have been misunderstood and really unpopular. When he got an award or was recognized in any way, he asked if she could be recognized alongside him. Often it was granted, but there were times his request was refused – and if so - he refused the recognition in return. He knew where and from whom his real, side by side, behind the scenes support came from – and was wise enough to acknowledge it. There was a smart man.

Behind every good and great man is a great woman? Yes - tis' still true – and the best men among us are aware of it. It is a truth recognized by those in the know from the beginning of time.

I know historically, for myself, that I am slower to come to certain realizations, not being as fast or perceptive as some of the women I have known. It has taken me weeks and years sometimes to really decipher the message I was given. How that makes me feel sad and stupid! I have missed things – only to find out she was saying something that I should have caught if I had been a wiser, better listener. In my ignorance I over-looked or misunderstood the message. The female language has been called by the term 'womaneze' because it almost seems like a mystery to some, like foreign speech at times. There are those who even say that we're from different planets, but I disagree. Some men unfortunately joke about the way women speak, but could it be that we laugh at what we don't understand and can't easily figure out? I think there is hope ahead. It is time for a far greater understanding to take place among all married men and women.

In these later years I have been growing through my mistakes. I am becoming wise enough to start asking for an explanation. God help us men to ask for a breakdown of the details when it all seems foreign and we don't understand what they are saying. It probably is important. And may the women in our lives be merciful enough to come to our rescue when we don't get it.

ↄ

With all this in mind, I have several short things to finish with here.

- My hope is that every man will find a woman who will be good to him and one that he will listen to. That means that we as men need to think beyond her beauty and ask ourselves if we respect her intelligence. Do you respect her thinking and opinions enough that you wouldn't want to live without her advice and counsel in your life? If not, stop. There are women out there that have these attributes. You need to take your only opportunity to choose the best woman you can find, one who will make a profound influence in your life.

- My hope is that every man will pay attention to the woman in his life, from the break of dawn to the end of the day. This may be an odd connection to this topic, but in an inadvertent way I recognized that my dog Peter was always happy to see me when I first came home. This is a pretty standard thing for a good dog, something which we all appreciate. I could be gone for an hour but he'd greet me at the door like it had been a year. But I also noticed two things about my response to him. If I went by him without stopping when he was there greeting me, wagging his tail and excited to see me, he wasn't that interested in further affection later on. Something was lost when I blew by him to do other things in our home. Conversely, if I stopped what I was doing when I first came in and spent a few moments with him, petting and rubbing his fur, his relationship with me was more bonded for the evening than if I had passed him by.

  Our wives deserve the same thing but in a more important human way. A few minutes in the morning being with her, a call during the day to tell her you're thinking of her, and a few minutes holding and kissing her when you come home goes a long way. This sets the tone for both of you during that day, and maybe for the rest of your life.

- May every man NOT feel like he is to lead alone; may he lead jointly together with his wife and, though dangerous to say to some, only pull rank if it is absolutely necessary for the situation at hand – absolutely necessary.

- May we as men understand that submission given by a woman is not to be enforced in a dominant way by a male, but it is an act of love and service between her and her God. It is for Him that she does this, and maybe it will flow down to you if you are humble and wise. Her support and love is a gift that is given to us by God Almighty. He is asking her to come along side us, to make us wiser and smarter. We need to be grateful for this gift and tell God how thankful we are for His care for us by treasuring her.

- May a man understand that his frustration with her at times may come from his lack of understanding of what she is talking about – and not the other way around. May he therefore be a good listener and ask her from several angles, if necessary, to explain what she is trying to say.
- May he be fortunate enough to win her friendship by treating her respectfully. If so, may she not give up on him but be willing to continue to help him and stand by him through the hard times.
- And may he value her enough to open his heart totally to her.

As it says in the book of wisdom,

'Who can find a virtuous and capable wife? She is more precious than rubies. Her *husband can trust her, and she will greatly enrich his life*. She brings him good, not harm, all the days of her life.'[5]

Notes

1. On Adam and God: unknown
2. The woman caught in adultery: The New Testament – John, chapter 8:3 – 11
3. On a woman of virtue: The Old Testament – Proverbs, chapter 31:13 – 21 [NLT]
4. Who her husband is because of her: The Old Testament – Proverbs, chapter 31:23, 28-29 [NLT]
5. Her effect on his life: The Old Testament – Proverbs, chapter 31:10-12 [NLT]

CHAPTER 3
Dating

Dating

"Dating is going somewhere you don't normally go, dressing like you don't normally dress and spending money you don't normally spend."

Lowell Burrier

Dating

"I don't need a friend who changes when I change and nods when I nod; my shadow does that much better."

Plutarch

Dating

My goal is to help all of us with principles that will strengthen and save our marriages when it seems like all is lost. At the very least I hope we will put our marriage troubles on hold until we have the answers or growth occurs. While traveling along this path I began to realize how important dating is to the purposes of marriage. I began to see the real impact of dating.

It's interesting to me that we don't have dating counselors. We have dating services, on line dating and dating sites – but I don't see professional or lay services where trained people are there to help you through this process. Maybe no one has thought of it yet. We wait until farther down the line to seek help from a professional marriage and family counselor when we're engaged and have already made the commitment, or after we've tied the knot. But it would be nice and a whole lot more helpful to seek counseling before this has happened. To this end, I would like to see someone put a shingle out someday that says, 'Dating, Marriage and Family Counseling'. I think the time has come.

Does dating get the proper and sober attention it rightly deserves in these days in which we live? How do I end up in a marriage without going through this important process? Unless my parents pick my spouse for me - I have to go through it. From what I can see, if you get dating *wrong* it will be harder to get marriage *right*. Other situations are bound to come into play that won't have a positive effect on your life. But if we get dating *right*, your marriage should be much more enjoyable.

Like baking bread, or some other recipe with detailed instructions and multiple ingredients, you don't skip steps if you want to make it right. If you skip steps or gloss over the details, you will either have to go back and start again or fumble with the mess you've made. Most of the problems of marriage that can also become issues of separation were details that were overlooked or not deemed important at the time you were dating. So let's give dating its due.

⤵

These are just suggestions for you to consider.

1. **Remember the goal of dating is not to get married, but to fall in love.**

I think we can turn dating into something akin to sport fishing. It's like we're off with a bunch of chum and charm. We have as our ultimate goal that of gaffing our best selection and then trying to land this choice tuna on the deck of our boat. Wrong idea. Marriage is not the goal, but giving and falling in love is. There is a huge difference between the two.

If we go through some changes and difficulties with the other person and take our time; if we learn about ourselves and what we have to improve; if we develop the skills of care and commitment, putting them to use in dating, if we become friends before becoming lovers, then marriage after finding love is just making it official.

But some get caught up in the catch and then start trying to figure out how to deal with what they've landed afterwards. It should be the other way around if you want marriage to be a place of happiness that has a bit of bliss mixed into it.

2. **Approach dating with the aspect of marriage in mind each time you go out.**

This may seem contrary to what I just said, but it is just a cautionary note on the flipside. I am just asking you to be selective up front about who you're dating and who you spend your time with.

People seem to get on your case if you get too 'marriage minded' when you go out with someone. I personally think you should be thinking of *eventual* marriage when you date – if not, you're going to open yourself up to trouble. Have a long term focus in mind and ask yourself up front, is this someone that I want to spend my life with? If you ask that simple question in the beginning, then you can spend time finding out if they're someone that you could love. You don't want to waste time looking at something you don't intend to take home. Worse yet, you don't want to take something home that you should have passed on.

So every date is a potential marriage partner – keep that thought in mind as you go forward - *please.*

3.   It's OK to shoot for the highest star.

I heard a well-known speaker say to some younger members of his congregation that they should not waste any more time but just get about the business of marrying and settling down. In that I'm afraid I didn't hear anything about being selective.

I think it's OK to find the best needle the haystack - for you. This is a lifetime decision. Pretty or handsome is good – you have to be attracted to them; smart is just as important, morals are essential, respect is necessary, the ability to earn money and handle it shows maturity, and having a clean dwelling combined with an orderly, neat appearance are characteristics that were always important to me. But you must decide for yourself.

I therefore recommend that you don't look at the clock. Understand yourself, think about what you really need vs. what you may want, enjoy the process and be as selective as you can. Keep it balanced by asking God to help you not miss what He has in mind for you. I think you'll be glad you did.

4. **Don't look for your clone.**

I think it's too easy to do this – finding our clone. We're kind of built to find the familiar in our world anyway but I think we should explore the options a bit more than we do.

In the computer dating world people often say 'I'm a vegan – I want someone who eats healthy like I do', and 'I bike, walk or kayak – looking for the same', or 'if you voted for Trump then we wouldn't be a good match'. These kinds of preferences may last a whole lifetime or they may change, but they're not the basis of love. Love is 'if you change, or regardless of what happens - I will still love *you*.' It's defined as a person's character and their qualities as a person, not what they drive, the size of their waist line, who they voted for, or the hobbies they pursue.

I remember my Uncle Bill and Aunt Rose when I ponder of this compatibility thing. Though they are gone they still give me so much encouragement when I think of them.

He was well over 6 foot and rugged like a tree stump – a man's man. I remember going out in Long Beach harbor with the family on their sailboat and Bill would practice man overboard drills with the kids. I'm sure they did a few dry runs prior to my being around before the real thing – but the day I was with them Bill would say, "Are you ready?" and then over the side he went. What kind of guy does that with the ocean water full of whatever that lurks beneath the surface and our being a half a mile away, or more, from the shore? It was part of why I remember him as being a man's man.

Rose was in good shape but she was small and very feminine, probably about 5' 4" at the most. I'm probably giving her a few extra inches even at that measurement, but she was a wonderful lady. Bill, as I said, was a force to be reckoned with, but not when Rose was around. I watched her say, "Now Bill . . ." in that lyrical voice of hers and his whole countenance changed. It just wasn't fair when she did that. He tried to put up a good fight most of the time to make it look good, but she really did have him from the start.

She was Catholic her whole life and faithfully, fervently so. Bill, although Anglican by background, wasn't much of anything along religious lines until the end of his life, but he loved her and was faithful to her. There were concerns from both sides of the family as to whether this whole thing would work. From the current 'dating site' perspective there was too much about them that just didn't match up. However, time proved them right. In my moments around them, I could see their love for each other even though they had all of this 'incompatibility'. They flourished because they did have a strong love and respect for each other. They were both going the same way in life, and their home and family reflected this.

I want the kind of love they had for each other, the love that overcomes hurdles and weathers storms. I think they also showed me how to handle differing viewpoints on faith and still keep love in place. A bit different than they were in this regard; I want a shared Christian faith in a partner, though we may still differ on the fine points. Overall however, like 'The Taming of the Shrew', give me a new perspective and different things to appreciate through my partner. I want to become a better man because of her and not just be satisfied with who I am today. If I am to change and adjust one more time, I just want to be molded by loving hands.

5. Get to know yourself.

The decisions we make will be defined by what we think and how much we know of ourselves. What are your strengths and weaknesses? What qualities do you bring into a relationship and what things do you need to improve? Are you needy or are you giving? Did you come from a healthy family experience or do you have a lot to learn about what a family means? Are you in a career that is satisfying to you, that uses your gifts and abilities, or are you looking for more fulfillment there too?

These questions are important to knowing where you are at and what kind of decisions you'd make if you moved toward something more serious with another. You might need to wait until you have better answers, or you may indeed be ready now to move forward.

6. **Talk a lot and get to know each other before you get involved in physical touch and kissing, but know that passion is also a healthy, necessary thing.**

Solomon's bride said,

"His left arm is under my head, and his right arm embraces me. Promise me, O women of Jerusalem, by the gazelles and wild deer, not to awaken love until the time is right"[1]

She talks here about intimacy and describes the passion of romantic touch. Along with this she gives the advice of being careful before stirring the more intimate side of a romantic relationship. When she says, "... do not awaken love until the time is right", this means to hold things in check until it is the proper next step in your relationship. You want to be secure in your care for each other before you kiss and hold each other close. Her advice is extremely wise. Be confident of who they are before that first kiss.

Know on the flipside that it's a healthy thing to have sexual feelings for the right person. If romantic feelings aren't there *somewhere*, if it isn't hard for you to resist holding them sometimes, then I think you are dating the wrong person. Just keep the ponies in check. Find out who they are and if it is love before this happens.

Bill Parish, in the movie 'Meet Joe Black', asks his daughter if she loves Drew, her steady companion. She expresses interest and respect for Drew, but her reactions over him isn't compelling enough for her father.

He confronts her about this. He tells her that he doesn't see an ounce of excitement in her about Drew. "It's not what you say about Drew," he says, "it's what you don't say. I want you to get swept away, I want you to levitate; I want you to sing with rapture and dance like a dervish. Yea . . . be deliriously happy – *at least leave yourself open to be.*"

"I know it's a cornball thing," he continues, "but love is passion, obsession, someone you can't live without. Because the truth is honey, there is no sense living your life without this. To make the journey and not fall deeply in love . . . well, you haven't lived a life at all. But you have to try, because if you haven't tried, you haven't lived."[2]

I won't elaborate here anymore because I'm sure you get his point. Just take the Shulamite woman's advice and have the more clear thinking taken care of before you stir up this kind of magic. And magic it is. Bill Parish would say that your toes should curl – when the time is right.

7. **Wait on commitment until you see them 'leak'.**

That's what Marce, the wife of one of my best friends, called it – 'leaking'.

What it means is if you like someone, date until something comes out in the other person that not a desirable trait. It may be just their humanness or their lack of maturity in an area where there should be more growth. Maybe it's a bad habit like picking your nose, some health issue, or a spout of momentary anger. Wait on this before making any long term commitments. She told me that it usually takes about 8 to 10 months for something like this to happen. I heard a woman say that her father-in-law wanted her and his son to wait 'through the seasons' [a year] before making a final decision to marry.

It doesn't mean that seeing a leak is a bad thing – you're going to 'leak' too. It's not just one sided. Leaking is an evaluation point that makes sure you're not just seeing someone through rose colored glasses. Will it be a major or minor issue when it happens? Will you like them enough to stay? Is it something that you can deal with or is it a tie breaker?

I like how this thing comes up in 'Meet Joe Black' again.

Joe Black lets Quince, one of my favorite characters in the story, know that he is a little confused about love.

"How do you know Allison loves you?" Joe asks Quince sincerely.

Quince pauses for a moment to think. "Because she knows the worst thing about me and it's OK," Quince replies. "It's like you know each other's secrets; the deepest, darkest secrets. Yea, and then you're free, free . . . you're free to love each other completely, totally – no fear. There's nothing you don't know about each other – and it's OK."

Words of wisdom.

Realize you don't want to bring your dump truck up into the driveway and drop the whole load on your first date. Getting to know someone is a gradual thing, just like peeling back an onion, as the donkey in Shrek says. There may be issues in your life you have to resolve privately or get counseling on before you bring them into the light for others to see. Some, for the benefit of others, may just yours to resolve alone.

Know that you don't have to go looking for flaws in the other person or dig around until you find *something*. Just wait it out. If you like them enough to hang around – the truths you need to know will come out eventually.

And at some point it will be OK to finally let down your guard. Your stumbles, your past, things you regret and all the mistakes that you have made, even during this relationship – to share them may be freeing for you. You'll now know if the acceptance you desire takes place between the both of you. If it's too much for one or the other of you, the relationship may end forever. There also may be a time apart between both of you while you mutually go off to find a greener pastures. You may realize later that there are others that have the same or worse problems – and you both may come back to this love you had together. And if its love for you and they leave, you might decide to wait things out on your own. They just have to be someone that you'd wait for.

8. Be able to live with each other's gifts or careers.

Steve Hinton Jr's family has been in aviation for years - but their passion for flying doesn't lie in the standard realm of the usual private airplanes you see at the airports around you. Theirs is not an everyday, normal brand of taking to the skies. They fly WWII aircraft that have been restored and modified.

Steve Jr has won the Reno Air Race 7 times and he is the youngest ever winner of that race, doing it at age 22. In a modified P-51 North American Mustang named 'Voodoo', he now holds the 3 Km record for having the fastest propeller driven aircraft in the world – a scorching 554.69 mph. His average speed over 4 runs was a monumental achievement of 531.53 mph. Though the younger Steve is obviously gifted for his craft, it is a risky business and dangerous passion that he pursues.

His father said, "This is serious business and I've been severely hurt. I broke my back and broke my legs when I crashed the Red Baron for instance, but I was young and I healed well."

In a documentary[3] on making his record speed run, Steve Jr said, "It's absolutely deafening inside this cockpit. You have an engine screaming loud in front of you, the cockpit is 140° inside, everything is shaking and vibrating in its own different way – why would you want to do something like this? The bottom line is every pilot wants to go fast. To break this record you have to be perfect. It's the pinnacle of aviation - only a few people have stood on top of this mountain."

The story of this young man is captivating to see, but what moved me as much was listening to his mom, Karen Hinton. "You know," she says, "it's funny being part of an aviation family. When Steve Sr. crashed the Red Baron it never even occurred to me to say 'don't fly.' You can't separate someone from their soul."

When watching her son go after the world speed record she echoed similar sentiments again. "As a mother you can't go through these kinds of things unaffected. You vibrate with every core of your being during these experiences. I don't want to watch him do this again and I know that's what they do. The blow the engine, they change it and they go again – and it's, ah, not going to be very easy to watch."

She had supported her husband and her son, both whom she loved, to pursue their calling – even though it may have left her a widow or a broken hearted mother. She bravely allowed them both to purse goals that were extremely risky because she knew how dear it was to both of them. Unlike some, she was fortunate to have gotten them both back alive. But there is a huge key to her choice that inspires me. Either way, she supported their gifts and passion. She took their risk too as part of her love for them.

I have to say here that there is a difference between spending too much time pursuing a hobby, at the family's expense, vs. pursing your gifts. Don't confuse the two. Karen knew that it was their passion and that they were among the best in the world at unlimited aircraft flying. She wasn't going to deny her son and her husband the right to pursue their dreams and follow what was imbedded into their souls. Some are just going after hobbies or pursuits they have no ultimate talent for. They should be finding and pursuing their gifts instead.

So, if your future husband or wife is going to work as a doctor, spending considerable hours in clinical work preparing for their profession, you need to be able to deal with this. If your husband is going to be on the SWAT Team for the police department, if she travels a lot for her job, if you both work odd hours or just have simple careers – can you live with this? If a spouse is in transition or willing to change occupations, then fine. But if it is their *gift* you are asking them to give up, then be careful – don't make them or yourself miserable. If you can't accept their calling and you expect them to change it, then you're being unreasonable. Get over it, or get on with your life by finding someone else.

9. Make God a priority – for both of you.

The Psalmist said, 'Unless the Lord builds a house, the work of the builders is wasted. Unless the Lord protects a city, guarding it with sentries will do no good.'[4]

Find a church, attend a home group where you will be known, but more than all of this – worship together in the privacy of your own home.

I believe private time with God, between you both, is more important than church. It isn't a substitute for gathering with others on a larger scale; it just is a closer look at the depth of your faith. You can be public with your faith when among others, but if you don't have it at home and in your private live, what you do in public doesn't matter. It is very important for God to be welcome in your home, and in your hearts, as you live together.

Notes

1. The Shulamite woman on physical intimacy: Song of Solomon 2:6 - [NLT]
2. Meet Joe Black: Universal Pictures, 1998
3. Steve Hinton Jr.: 'Five Thirty Five' / Racing against the odds in a WWII plane [YouTube]
4. God building a home: Psalms 127:1 [NLT]

CHAPTER 4

Love

Love

'Set me as a seal upon your heart, as a seal upon your arm; for love is as strong as death, passion fierce as the grave.

Its fires of desire are as ardent flames, a most intense flame. Many waters cannot quench love, neither can floods drown it. If a man offered for love all the wealth of his house, it would be utterly condemned.'

Solomon
Song of Songs 8:6 – 7
Modern English Version

Love

'Many claim to have unfailing love, but a faithful person who can find?'

Solomon
Proverbs 20:6
New International Version

Love Never Dies

I remember being on a plane, coming back from a business trip late at night. I sat next to a gentleman on the plane for nearly the whole trip without saying anything. This was an unusual thing for me because I'm talkative – but it was the last leg of a long flight and it was late. The cabin was dark, I was tired and he probably was too.

Being talkative, I've listened to everything I've ever heard myself say in life several times over. I didn't want to bore myself and possibly someone else by just the same old small talk again. It didn't seem like there was much to offer the person next to me this time of night anyway. Eventually, when we saw the lights of our destination city coming into focus below and people started to mill about, I decided at the end to break the ice at least a bit.

I may have asked if he was from Spokane or if his wife was waiting for him at the airport. I don't remember what the opener was after all this time, but we were soon talking about wives and marriage. With not many minutes left before coming into the pattern for landing, he showed me a picture of his wife from her business card. In the picture I saw an educated, professional woman who looked very capable in her career pursuit. I asked him how long he been married. I remember from his response that it seemed like a short period of time given his age.

"First marriage?" I asked.

"No," he replied, and went on to say that he had been married to his high school sweetheart before this but things didn't work out as planned. I told him that I was truly sorry that his first marriage hadn't succeeded.

In the many times I have run into divorced people and asked about their first marriage, their responses rarely move me. I seem to live in a world where people have no love anymore for their previous spouses – like it completely disappeared with the wind. There are comments about the former spouse that come out – usually never flattering – that make you wonder why they ever married them in the first place. He, however, was different. His words just moments before we landed still remain with me today.

I wish I could remember his name or face – I cannot. I am just glad, now looking back, that I had broken the ice. It was truly worth the few minutes we shared.

Still holding his new wife's business card he said, "You know, my new wife is pretty and I tell her so every day. I make sure that I appreciate her and I do what I need to do to let her know that I love her and will take care of her." He seemed like he was sensitive and considerate of her as the new person in his life. Then he paused for what seemed like a long moment. "But," he said, and I still hear him say this to this day, "there isn't a day that goes by where I don't think of my first wife."

I was stunned by the honesty that he chose to share with me. Such words and openness have been too rare in my journey through life. I think I know what our Lord meant when He heard the words of the Centurion and said, in essence, "I tell you, I haven't see faith like this in all Israel."[1]

What did my friend on the plane mean?

I've talked to people about this story and they think that it's terrible that he still thought of his former wife – like maybe he should have never gotten married to the new one since he had these feelings. Some thought he was cheating on her by looking back to the past. But I think there is a deeper truth to his comment. I certainly didn't see his feelings as cheating and I don't think he is alone in his situation.

In a Hallmark book on love[2] where participants had to have at least 50 years of marriage, one husband talked about his marriage that lasted for this amount of time and more. He spoke some words of truth that relate to our man on the plane, as well as many other people. He referred to 1 Corinthians 13 in the New Testament where it says that love never dies – saying is it there, be it ever so small, whether you sense it or not.

Most feel like love comes from us; that its very existence goes up and down with our lack of faith or ever changing emotions. But what if that's not true; what if love has a life of its own? When we fall in love, then fall out of love, it appears that we didn't nurture it properly and it died. But the scriptures say that,

> 'Prophesy and speaking in unknown languages and special knowledge will become useless. But love will last forever!'[3]

Would it surprise you if your love for a previous spouse, that you thought was over, still resides within your heart? What do you do when you are with someone else now and you come to that realization? That's what I was listening to and why my friend on the plane is not alone in his statement – he was just honest enough to say it out loud.

Michael, one of my lifetime best friends, gave me some insight on this.

He said some divorced people go through the awkward situation, over and over again, of being at family occasions and events where their former spouse turns out to be present as well. It feels like the same old feeling when the former partner walks into the room, and you're disturbed because you thought the whole thing was over between you both years ago. But here it is again, that funny feeling that rises up inside your chest. "What is wrong with me?" you think. You may be angry with yourself and full of resolve to never let this feeling come over you again. But it still happens 10, 20, 30 years down the road from a broken marriage – and goes on 'till the end of your life.

Realize it is not *you* per se', it is your *heart*. Love has a life of its own.

Your heart goes out to make the connection with your former spouse because it recognizes where it belongs. It makes a bee line toward home. Your heart takes off running before your mind can shout to it, "Hey, we don't live there anymore." Somewhere in this process, as if you are watching it happen in slow motion, you will see this take place. It is like a bird hitting a transparent window; your independent heart will realize it's being shunned and it will turn around. Your heart will return back into your chest, a little hurt, wondering why it's instincts were right but still having to suffer rejection all over again.

That's also why divorce is called the problem of 'a hardened heart.' The rejecting person feels the advance too, but they push it aside and turn those feelings off – as best as they can.

So realize in that moment that there is nothing wrong with *you* or your heart. This feeling inside of you only indicates that the heart was right. For what is supposedly gone forever really isn't; and you both should actually be together - even if that is a dim or deserted memory.

Essentially, this is what was going on within my friend on the plane. I don't know the circumstances, but I do know that the love he felt in his heart for his first wife was never going to die. The loss and the feeling of pain and sorrow can be an enduring, lifelong hurt. This is why we need to hold on, even when it seems like everything between you has disappeared. To hold on and wait is going to be a major theme of this book.

So as we talk about love, please don't find yourself in a place or a situation where you've given up, only finding out later that your heart didn't give up with you. Wait and allow God to work - even if it isn't on your time table. He isn't done yet, and He alone is the only One who can do impossible things.

Notes

1. Jesus and the Centurion: Luke 7:1-10 [NLT]
2. Married For Life – 2004 by Honor Books exclusively for Hallmark Cards Inc.
3. Love never fails: 1 Corinthians 13:8 [NLT]

Love - Letting William Tell

Love as spoken of in 1 Corinthians 13 is probably known to many of us. In those words that Paul was inspired to pen, he spoke of love suffering long and yet being able to be kind. He addressed how love isn't self-seeking but really cares more for others. He says ultimately, through all things, love will never fail.

This is a seemingly impossible gauntlet that God throws down, but it is really the quality in life that we want the most. To love others and to be loved in return, without losing the ability to care and have the companionship of those who are the most important to us, this is our most endearing need. It is so important to know that God stands behind all this and demonstrates this also in His unfailing love towards us.

Shakespeare's Sonnet 116 however is a literary work that we may not be as familiar with. These words William Shakespeare penned on love are amazingly eloquent in my opinion. I feel, in the human realm of inspiration where we are thankful for the gifts God has given to men, I've not found words of such beauty and truth on love as these that he penned.

I would like to look at his Sonnet and let William give us his take on love as we look at this subject. He does such a good job, indeed.

Sonnet 116

Let me not to the marriage of true minds admit
impediments;
Love is not love which alters when alteration finds, or
bends with the remover to remove.
O no, it is an ever fixed mark, that looks on tempests and
is never shaken;
It is the star to every wandering bark, whose worth's
unknown, though his height be taken.
Love's not Times fool, though rosy lips and cheeks
within his bending sickles compass come,
Love alters not with his brief hours and weeks, but bears
it out even to the edge of doom;
If this be error and upon me be proved, I never writ, nor
no man ever loved.

William Shakespeare
April 23, 1564 – April 23, 1616

It seems to me like there are a host of seen and unseen voices about us, whispering their contrary and deceiving ideas about how love works, and doesn't work, into our ears. These voices can affect people and the culture around us often times in very harmful ways.

Part of this deceit is driven by negative statements from the mouths of those that speak on love based on their poor experiences; maybe their poor attitudes as well. There are also the marriage statistics predicted in magazines, the opinions of various sociologists and psychologists, the philosophies on love voiced in popular songs, and even what your parent, aunt, uncle, or friend thinks.

Like the 3D glasses we use at the movies, I think we'd be surprised at the myriad of elements, coming at us from sources all around us, which attempt to confuse the way we look at real love.

1. *'Let me not to the marriage of true minds admit impediments'*

Admitting impediments into the equation we call love relates to these voices I've described before. Why would people want to lead us into error or spin webs of deception on things of the heart? I don't know. Love is just too important to twist, confuse or mess with.

I believe when William Shakespeare looked at love he understood that there is confusion, and therefore some collateral damage that surrounds the subject. I appreciate that he was not only a great playwright, but I can also see he was someone who apparently cared a great deal about people. Shakespeare used his station in life to reach out to us on this matter. He knew that lovers holding hands and the lives they will want to share is an important, precious thing. It was to still the voices and silence as much of the confusion as he could that he wrote these lines to us on love. Though using a play on words, he sincerely wanted to put nothing between the 'marriage of true minds' on this key subject in life.

His statement about admitting or allowing impediments is the equivalent to me of, "I don't want to put out any bad information that would lead you astray or cloud your thinking." He didn't want his life, his thoughts, or his words to hinder our being able to find or give real love. He meant for his thoughts to be pure, true and straight to the target, like an arrow shot from the long bow of his day. His desire was to help us to find what we wanted most in life – this precious thing called love.

2. *'Love is not love which alters when alteration finds, or bends with the remover to remove; O no, it is an ever fixed mark, that looks on tempests and is never shaken.'*

Alterations and changes in life, they are always bound to happen. Maybe that's why the traditional marriage vows contain the statement, 'for better or worse, in sickness and in health, for richer or poorer, 'till death do us part.' These words reflect a practical, historical understanding of life and what it can offer us at times. We want the better, but we need the assurance that someone will be there during the worst. There will be twists in the road, dips into uncertain valleys - things we least expect or desire – but we hope to be a faithful companion during these times.

If we choose to love a partner based upon temporary things like similar activities, sports team affiliations, compatible political views or common food consumptions – then something changes – we're stuck. What if your spouse wakes up one day and wants to pursue a different interest? What if they no longer like golf, or whatever else you have done together anymore? Maybe they're in an accident or impaired in some way. Now the trips you always took and the breadth of activities you had planned together for the future could be mildly to severely derailed. If these activities are what your relationship was based on, your shallow vessel is going to take on water fast. Sadly, you will see this temporary kind of criteria for compatibility listed on dating sites all the time. "I do this, this and this – do you?" This is not personally where I want to be.

The love we want to develop is not that of finding our clone, it is one that we hope will transcend all differences and situations. We should care for the person we love, regardless of what they are or aren't. It will be a *giving* love that we will offer, centered on what we can be, do, or provide for another. Real love doesn't alter, as he says, and it doesn't bend - in the face of high emotions, arguments, difficulties, changes, and new circumstances - because it is deeper and stronger than all of this.

This concept of *giving* love more than we *get* love may make all the difference in our lives. I believe all great lovers had *giving* as a key element of their relationship toward one another. Conversely, those who want to take from one another and only give back on the basis of what they get in return are possibly not ready for a relationship. Just because I can put a ring on someone's finger doesn't mean that I understand what I should do and be for someone else's sake.

'But don't use your freedom to satisfy your sinful nature. Instead, use your freedom to serve one another in love. For the whole law can be summed up in this one command: 'Love your neighbor as yourself.'[1]

The whole idea of providing a giving love to another is the reverse of what we think love should be. But the love we so desperately desire comes from our ability to grow and think of others. It also comes from a decision we make to give it to another, regardless of what we get back.

This ultimately means that if someone does an about-face, you don't do a 'tit for tat' and match their actions. Sure you're hurt, and it is no fun when your world caves in, but did you love them? That is the question – before and after. There were 2 people in the relationship and 2 at the altar. Did you mean your part of what was said regardless of the other person's commitment? If so, even when they are now showing that they did not love you, hold on to your decision about them. Embrace it – even though in times like this it will feel like hugging a porcupine. It will make you a better person to know that your love didn't bend back like theirs did. You will be a better candidate for love to happen again if they don't come back.

It also teaches you about hurt and the depth of your commitment when you're faced with this kind of a challenge. Loving in the face of adversity enlarges your heart – increasing your capability to love again.

It is interesting that most people that haven't been through divorce and the loss of a marriage think that both people wanted out. It appears from the outside that there is such a thing as an amicable divorce most of the time, but these conditions are rare. It is more commonly true than not, that for every person that left a marriage there is one that didn't want them to go. Therefore there is such a thing as a jilted spouse showing true love in the face of a host of difficulties. There are those who display a steadfast heart that was unmoving – even in the face of tough circumstances.

I will throw this in for balance. I believe an unconditional love should have conditions. The conditions it will ask for won't have anything to do with the depth of its assurance or commitment, but it will have everything to do with the relationship. I will cover this again perhaps – but let it suffice to say that if you love someone you care about their conduct. You don't withdraw your love or commitment to them, but it may be right to withdraw your relationship until their actions change. It is confusing to me when I see people who think that 'to love' means they must endorse whatever behavior their loved one puts out. This is especially glaring to me when parents put up with any kind of gross behavior that comes from their children, but can't tolerate a spouse who steps out of line as much as an inch. I hear people say, "But it is different with my kids."

Really? How? Let's talk about that sometime.

3. 'It is the star to every wandering bark, whose worth's unknown, though his height be taken.'

Behind President John Kennedy's desk in the Oval Office, inscribed in a block of wood, was the old Breton 'Fisherman's Prayer'. It said, 'O, Thy sea is so great and my boat is so small.' How true – the ocean is vast. I've been out on the sea beyond the sight of land for many days during my years in the US Navy and it was like walking in an endless Kansas wheat field.

In Shakespeare's day a 'bark' was vessel. His use of it in this Sonnet was to illustrate a ship or a boat out at sea, possibly lost or wandering about. The word 'bark' is an analogous term for a person like you and I, trying to find our way through life, needing some guidance and direction from above.

Realize that a ship far out at sea doesn't have a view of the shoreline or the guidance of the city lights in the distance to guide its way. Though things are different today with satellite navigation, for most of history your only bearing out on the vast ocean was the stars above and possibly the sextant in your hands. If you were adrift, with no knowledge of how to read the stars or how to understand this little instrument you held in your hands, you truly would be wandering aimlessly.

A sextant will take information from the location of the stars and give you the direction and the distance that you've traveled. But though a sextant can guide your way it can't help you understand the magnificence of what you see in the stars above. That instrument cannot explain how they hang in space without visible support, why they twinkle as they do and how they maintain their orbits so precisely. And it's not just the sea goers; we land folks look up at night but usually do not understand their value either.

This is true about the other things of nature that surround us too. There are glorious things going on all about us that we don't understand, but we have just have just gotten used to them.

My brother Rick talked to me about maple tree seeds that spin to the ground, sailing away from the mother tree, using their aerodynamic abilities to find other locations to root. I've seen them do this since I was just a kid.

He had been pondering his question for some time before springing it on me; I could tell. "Do you think maple trees have eyes?" he said.

"No - certainly not," I replied, wondering where he was going.

"Then how did the maple tree figure out that it needed aerodynamics," he said, "to make its seeds twirl in the air - so they could spin greater distances away in order to find open places to grow? How did the maple tree know about height and what air was? How did it know about distance and the need for it? And once the seed left the tree, how would it know, without sight, whether its mutation was beneficial or not?"

Silence for a moment. I was a bit dumbfounded by these questions that made it clear I had not been paying attention. I had never thought about all of this, though the process had been in front of my eyes since birth. I had *seen* many maple seeds travel, but I had not *understood* their true value and what their design meant.

The seraphim said, "The earth is full of His glory"[2], but we don't see it like we should. Since we have come into the world as infants all these glorious things like the ocean and maple seeds have been here from the start. By continual association with them since birth we have lost our ability to wonder – so we take obvious, miraculous, every day things all around us for granted. There are so many aspects of this wonderful world that can be scientifically measured, charted and graphed, but whose true worth and story still remain unknown to the heart that doesn't wonder.

I think it's the same way with love – it is such a key thing in life. We think we understand a few things about the heart and how to navigate through a relationship, but there is more to love than this. If we understood love better as we should, and knew of its true value and power, we should cherish it as one of the most important things in life.

4. *'Love's not Times fool, though rosy lips and cheeks within his bending sickles compass come, Love alters not with his brief hours and weeks, but bears it out even to the edge of doom;'*
I think this is pretty straight forward.

When the hair goes bad, the teeth get sparse and wobbly, and your spouse's frame starts to bend a bit with age, are you are still with your close companion and the one you love?

I think during courtship we may need to consider what someone might look like when they get older. It might help our thinking a bit. Like Belle in The Beauty and the Beast, could you love this person when the whole outside has been changed?

I think of Christopher Reeves, telling his wife after his paralyzing accident that she was free to go, but she stayed.

Mark Twain also loved his wife for a lifetime. On the death of Olivia, Twain said, "I am a man without a country. Wherever Livy was, that was my country."[3]

5. 'If this be error and upon me be proved, I never writ, nor no man ever loved.'

Shakespeare throws himself on the altar of sacrifice at the end, saying some pretty strong words about his convictions and his abilities. He wrote beautifully – of this there is no question - so this part of the line about his not being a writer is obviously not true. But he emphasizes what he did at the beginning – that love and its existence isn't in question, we are. At least I, for one, agree. There are those among us (I count myself to be one) who do not fully understand yet what they need to know about love. So many don't and the decisions of their life reflect it.

But I want to. For you and I, and the people we know who don't have the kind of love that he pens about here, there is hope and room for growth. We just haven't loved as we should yet.

Encompassing His journey here on earth and His experience with us as humans, Jesus said, "Forgive them Father for they know not what they do."[4] He knew something deeply troubling about us – that we don't have the answers we need by ourselves and that problems were going to come to the surface because of all this. It's not that the answers don't exist, or that they're way off in space out of our reach; we just will need God's help to find our way through life.

I want to believe that if more people understood, that in a few months or years they would have the marriage answers that elude them today, that they might stop in times of crisis and just take a breath – wait. If people could challenge themselves to seek to be what they need to be, instead of looking for the answers in their spouse, things could change for the better. If they knew what it was that they were bringing upon themselves, when in frustration they started to destroy the tie that binds, I hope they would stop their collision course with heartbreak. Just stop what they are doing and take a rest until the true answer arrives. Ask for help from above. Prayer would be very appropriate at these times.

And if they knew how much they would regret later on in life their decision to leave a marriage or a relationship, I hope there would be more hearts willing to stay and be changed in the present moment.

Notes

1. On a giving love: Galatians, chapter 5:13 – 14 [ESV]
2. The earth is full of His glory: Isaiah 6:3
3. On the death of Olivia Langdon Clemens: Mark Twain - in a letter to her brother.
4. Jesus' words from the cross – "Forgive them Father . . .": Luke 23:34

1 Corinthians 13

'If I could speak all the languages of earth and of angels, but didn't love others, I would only be a noisy gong or a clanging cymbal. If I had the gift of prophecy, and if I understood all of God's secret plans and possessed all knowledge, and if I had such faith that I could move mountains, but didn't love others, I would be nothing. If I gave everything I have to the poor and even sacrificed my body, I could boast about it; but if I didn't love others, I would have gained nothing.

Love is patient and kind. Love is not jealous or boastful or proud or rude. It does not demand its own way. It is not irritable, and it keeps no record of being wronged. It does not rejoice about injustice but rejoices whenever the truth wins out. Love never gives up, never loses faith, is always hopeful, and endures through every circumstance.

Prophecy and speaking in unknown languages and special knowledge will become useless. But love will last forever!'

Paul
1 Corinthians 13:1 – 8
New Living Translation [NLT]

CHAPTER **5**

The Man for All Seasons

"Your approval means nothing to Me, because I know you don't have God's love within you. For I have come to you in my Father's name, and you have rejected Me. Yet if others come in their own name, you gladly welcome them. No wonder you can't believe! For you gladly honor each other, but you don't care about the honor that comes from the one who alone is God."

Jesus
John 5:41 - 44
NLT – New Living Translation

The Man for All Seasons

'Wisdom shouts in the streets. She cries out in the public square. She calls to the crowds along the main street, to those gathered in front of the city gate . . . . "Come and listen to my counsel. I'll share my heart with you and make you wise."'

Proverbs 1:20 - 23
NLT – New Living Translation

The Man for All Seasons

I think it is important to the things to come after this chapter, and essential for life as we live it, to get one critical detail firmly understood. So much hinges upon it – and it is this.

Jesus is the most central figure in history; this is without debate. Whether you're religious or not, whether you're from Africa, Australia, Russia or downtown New York City, to even argue over this is ridiculous.

If you believe in Him but are weak in your faith or not eloquent at all, it is of no real issue. The events surrounding Him speak so loudly that there is very little required on your part actually; yours is mostly to only bear witness to what you know about Him and to give words to what He has personally done for you. Know that with or without you, He is as sure as the days, dates and marking of time. Even the calendar bears witness to His entry into history, roughly 2020 years ago as of this writing.

It surprises me when I hear of people who don't 'believe' in Jesus. Or, they did, but they don't 'believe' in Him anymore. Maybe it's a misunderstanding of terms and words. What did they believe in to begin with? Did they believe in their ability to just have an intellectual experience when trying to understand Him, or was their belief in the emotions they were having, hoping that this would guide them? Was it in their church, its social order and the beliefs that unified their gathering together with others that held their allegiance?

I also understand in a general sense that there are those who want the freedom to not acknowledge Him, to not follow Him, to blot Him out and keep Him from interrupting their agenda. But if by saying 'we don't believe in Him' means we do *not* believe that He existed . . . that's not one of the actual, available, intellectual options any of us have. Thinking on this level has to be on the same floor where the Flat Earth Society meets. I'm not being condescending; I'm presenting a valid and important point.

The essence of Christianity is not driven by my intellect, my church or my emotions, but it is the person of Jesus, the Jewish Messiah (also called the Christ in Greek[1]) that is at its core. Personally, I think we get the whole religious thought process muddled up in experiences, emotions and subjective thinking, while the facts go wanting for a home.

Maybe the crux of this issue may be from the confusion that swirls around the word 'faith'.

In some cases, to certain people, the term faith means, "You'll just have to take my word for it . . . . because that's what I believe!" This can be a prevalent statement for most of the general public on anything – especially when it comes to discussing any hard evidence over the essential points of their beliefs.

In Christianity, the use of the word 'faith' is different and should be understood as so. It doesn't mean that you have to take my word for it or anyone else's for that matter. What it means is that in Christianity the details are solid; the only 'faith' required is to just acknowledge that I wasn't there, in person, at the time the events took place. The documentation of the events are definite, the locations spoken of are there and can be visited, there were plenty of eyewitnesses – but the only caveat is that I just wasn't there to validate it all with my own eyes. I wasn't present at the time the events took place and neither was anyone else that is alive today. But the facts are as real as anything else in history. This is the 'faith' that is required to believe in Him then, and also the obstacle to overcome if I choose to not believe in Him as well.

The Christian idea of faith is similar to a belief in the existence of George Washington, Napoleon or Caesar. I wasn't there when all these men had their moments on the stage of history – but the facts are pretty verifiable that they lived. I can see Mt. Vernon, wander through the halls of France, or visit the ruins of Italy today. I can find records on these men that show of their existence, art work that acknowledges them and documents that record the accomplishments that they left on the marks of history. I can find references to eyewitnesses in the annals of the historical records that say they saw them, talked with them and recorded their utterances. Am I absolutely 100% sure that they existed? I would say yes, I am *about* 100% sure, but I have to admit that *I didn't see it with my own eyes.* I lack the absolute certainty of being there, and so it goes for you too. I can't take you back in time to shake their hands, introduce ourselves to them, and say with finality as I turn to you, "See, here they are!" But the evidence is overwhelming on the side of almost 100% absolute certainty.

It is the same with many of the things we believe. The origins of matter, mankind, the earth and the universe are other examples of faith. I believe personally in the special creation by God of all we see and maybe you believe in the evolution of matter that was eternally existent. We both should have our best and most logical facts at hand to support our beliefs, but it still remains that neither of us were there when it happened. It is our belief, one way or the other, at the end of the day that we have. But we lack the absolute, empirical, scientific evidence - that can be viewed over and over again in a laboratory or mixed up time and time again in a test tube – to show how it all began. This is the very reason that some of these topics get so heated when being discussed.

One of my favorite references to this concept of faith having a solid core to it is when Paul the Apostle had to stand trial in

Caesarea before Festus and Agrippa, verifiable men of that time. This historical account is in the Book of the Acts of the Apostles[2].

Paul was standing and talking before these two, real, notable men of history, both who lived close enough to the timeline of the events surrounding Jesus of Nazareth to easily verify the 100% authenticity of what Paul was saying. The fact that Paul was even there standing before them was due to his faith in this Jesus of Nazareth. If there was no Jesus, what were Festus and Agrippa wasting their time over? What were the Jewish leaders so upset about, and why was Paul willing to be standing there on trial? In similar, analogous terms, coming from our own American history, who was our colonial army following and who were the thousands of British soldiers fighting against if there was no George Washington? What famous President and General did John Adams, Thomas Jefferson and the entire Continental Congress refer to if George Washington wasn't a real person? There is no difference between these two references.

So here, Paul refers to this key aspect of a correct faith in one of my most favorite verses, and he outlines the most important thing about having a faith that is credible. He tells of it to both Festus and King Agrippa.

He said,

> "I am fortunate, King Agrippa, that you are the one hearing my defense today against all these accusations made by the Jewish leaders, for I know you are an expert on all Jewish customs and controversies. Now please listen to me patiently!"

As Paul related historical events about this notable figure of Jesus that represented Christianity, it says that one of the leaders before him had an unusual reaction.

Suddenly Festus shouted, "Paul, you are insane. Too much study has made you crazy!"

Festus was no doubt embarrassed that Paul was talking about his Christian faith before his guests, in the same way that some would be today. It says much about this person of Jesus, and we will look into this in just a moment. The text goes on to say,

'But Paul replied, "I am not insane Most Excellent Festus. What I am saying is the sober truth. And King Agrippa knows about these things. I speak boldly, for I am sure these events are all familiar to him, *for they were not done in a corner!*"

This then is the key item to a real faith; the facts and events that surround a proper faith *should not have been done in some obscure corner. They must be solid and verifiable* - and not, in the end, just be based on your 'strong' feelings or emotions. There is no foundation to emotional or feeling faith – it is usually understood to really be a 'blind faith'.

It's interesting that in my studies of other religions, so many details are shaky, shady, not verifiable, and done behind closed doors - ultimately visible to only a select few. It is important that you be sure that you can trust that what you believe is *true*.

The facts here were clear - and Agrippa was well acquainted with what had been going on regarding the events of Jesus of Nazareth's life. Within a few short years the Roman Empire, of which America pales in comparison to, was going to be turned upside down by the words, life and news of the resurrection of Jesus. So what 'not done in a corner' in this sense means is that on one of the greatest stages in history, when there was one Empire with one common language, with historical records kept, excellent roads to travel on and a sea safe from pirates; when the safety of your travel was guaranteed by a vast Roman army – Jesus arrived on the scene for all to see. And Paul carried this message of Jesus' life to the farthest reaches of this Empire.

Why would a Roman Empire quake, shake and change over a fabricated story that could easily be exposed and debunked in its day? The facts here are equal to anything in history, if not more so, and are as good as any get. It is not logical to put this kind of evidence alongside a guru on the far reaches of nowhere, a person that may have lived years ago but the records are fuzzy, a religious leader that everyone wants to embellish but also cover up the real facts about, or a presumed miraculous event that only 5 people were present for. No – this was different on a scale of 1 billion to 1. These historical events changed the way we have marked the calendar for over 2,000 years – and still going strong. It is a faith that is different from fairy-tales.

This is why when someone says they 'don't believe in Jesus', I think they've mixed things up a bit. Is turning our back on obvious historical references the route we have determined to take? Was my faith centered around churches and creeds that I used to approve of and not on Jesus? Was it based on the solemn practices or festivals I used to adhere to that now I do not? All of these external things are trinkets and tinsel, ornaments on a Christmas tree, but the real substance of any Christian faith is in this person of history, Jesus of Nazareth.

Will Durant, on his history of Roman civilization[3] asks the question of 'did Christ exist?' He reflects that for the fishermen and common people that followed Jesus, for them to come up with a character like Him with a life that is so real and not fake, would be a larger miracle than the one that is presented to us.

In the same way, I have often thought of what I would say if you dragged an adulterous woman before me and said, "So what are you going to do here . . . ?" I could have never in a million years with a thousand typewriters come up with, "Let him who has no sin throw the first stone." If you brought to me the question of, "Who shall we serve – Caesar or God?", it would have never occurred to me to ask you to bring me a coin, point to the face that was on it, and say to you, "Give unto Caesar what's Caesars and give to God what's Gods." If I had, I would have just described, in a profoundly simple fashion, the role of society, the government and the church in less than 15 words. If I gave you from His appearance until now, you couldn't have come up with this stuff yourself either, let alone 12 guys from a basic Israeli background 2,000 years ago. I agree with Durant – you just can't make Him up; nor the writings about this man that has impacted more lives and more nations than any other person or book ever.

⌇

To be fair to others, Jesus is not the only notable figure in history however and He is not oblivious to this. Other belief systems may tell you to toss everyone and everything overboard if it is not tied into their central figure or their thinking, but Christianity is not like this. Jesus didn't have this type of requirement on His list. We can have our mentors, sports heroes, our historical figures, political examples and native national leaders – He understands and expects this I believe. I am sure that He hopes all of us will choose individuals to admire that are truly worthy of honor and are good examples for ourselves and our children, but the whole issue of there being other significant people in history is not a point of conflict for Him.

He would just simply say that we should give proper honor where honor is due.

So, when you're talking about soccer and Pelé, Caesar and Rome, Jack or Tiger, Mickey Mantle and baseball, surfing and Laird Hamilton, New Zealand and the America's Cup, Roger Bannister and the 4 minute mile, or your favorite [honorable] American President – give the rightful kind of honor to these people that is due them. And in the same way, Jesus would ask you to give Him His rightful honor too.

And what is His rightful honor? This is a question that possibly ties in with another. If Jesus *is* the most central figure in history you ask, where is all the honor that should be given to Him? Why isn't He regarded as the most key person in history by all of the world's population?

It's a simple answer. His rightful place is denied Him by many because of what was told about Him. It is because of what He did, what He said and who He is.

He said that He was God come to mankind. A star shown over his birth place, and angels, shepherds and kings bowed before Him when He was an infant. He spoke words that we had not heard before, nor have we heard since. He accepted, and even expected, to be worshiped by all of mankind. He said that He alone was the way to Heaven, to God the Father, and that all other beliefs in contradiction to these truths were false.

And lastly, He rose from the dead. He separates Himself even further from all the others you know by this singular event, for they are buried and gone - but He is not. I've often thought that if someone didn't believe this, then have them go to Jerusalem today. Ask anyone you can find to tell you where He is *still* buried and tell me exactly what they say to you. May I suggest ahead of time that regardless of their religious affiliation, all of them will probably wonder where you are from that these events have escaped your notice. They may laugh at your question. The tomb He was laid in remains empty to this day and *that is well known.*

Notice that the other notable figures of history don't ask as much either – and that's why we can enjoy them with such ease. Jesus, however, asks to be the most important person in your life and will take nothing less. If only He could be a bit more reasonable! But then He wouldn't be Jesus, and He wouldn't be God come to man. It is because of this; who He is, what He did, and what He expects - that the casual, middle ground that we as people would rather have gets destroyed.

So, in and among all the difficulties you may have with all of this that surrounds Him, I hope you can work your way through it and come out the other side – successfully. However, win or lose, He still remains the most central figure in human history.

This will always be without debate.

Notes

1. Christ: The New Testament – John, chapter 1:41 [NLT – New Living Translation]
2. Paul's testimony in front of Festus and Agrippa: The New Testament – The Book of Acts, chapter 26:24-36 [NLT]
3. Caesar and Christ; A History of Roman Civilization and of Christianity from their beginnings to A.D. 325 [Simon and Schuster, New York: 1944]

CHAPTER 6

Marriage

Marriage

'Lord, who may dwell in Your sacred tent? Who may live on Your holy mountain?

The one whose walk is blameless, who does what is righteous, . . who keeps an oath even when it hurts and does not change their mind.'

David
Psalms 15:1-4
New International Version [NIV]

Marriage

"A good marriage is the union of two good forgivers"

Mark Twain

The Angels Stand Before God

One day the angels came to present themselves before the Lord, and Satan came with them. He was once a part of this angelic host, doing good things, but a lot had changed since then.

As they gathered into this present assembly, Satan predictably stood alone. It was far more than not being the crowd favorite. To be near him, or in association with him, was beyond dangerous. It was known to all assembled this day that he had caused many of their fellow former angelic friends to fall. Many of them were still remembered and their absences felt.

He had come alone, as usual. His minions, demons and sub-devils were never invited, nor allowed, to travel and come to these gatherings.

There were several reasons for this.

First, he wasn't a nice guy – plain and simple.

Second, he didn't want these former angels to remember how good it was before they left. Leave best (or worst) alone he thought – don't expose the deck to being shuffled again. Having them looking back and thinking about the past, looking in the rear view mirror again so to speak, was going to open up to too many problems. He didn't want to deal with a possible dissention, nor take any chances on their being upset.

He needed a following; his ego was one that demanded it. It would therefore be too much for him to not have his own little kingdom. More like a captive audience is how you might describe those who were his followers though. For those in his kingdom it was like living in several of the countries we know of today; countries where you are locked in and freedom is locked out. It is the same as certain territories we know of that have border walls, wire fences, and sentries at their posts who kept their *own* people from leaving. As the head of this fragile, shallow kingdom – Satan kept them under fear and suppression as he couldn't stand the obvious outcome of losing everybody.

Those who worked for him really didn't have any time off – they were to be about weaving their deceitful tasks. There was no such thing as a day of rest once a week, something that God cooked up because He cared about His subjects. Those in Satan's service had no holidays. All duties carried immediate punishment if not carried out swiftly and correctly. Time was short and he had a job to do. Just as it was in his own kingdom, his earthly goal was to confuse or turn as many humans away from God as he could.

Lastly, those under his command wouldn't have wanted to come. Unlike him, they didn't have the boldness to actually come face to face with God anymore – especially after all that had transpired in the past.

⌒

His reputation, known far and wide, was an odd and sort of funny thing to him. In the deception of mankind, he thought himself to be a bit over-rated. From everything everyone else said, evil things were always made out to be totally his fault. But in reality, based upon his own experience, it was the humans that were the most responsible for their problems. Satan observed over the years that they brought the wood to build the bonfire – he just brought the matches. It was their error of not listening to God, not his total intervention into the affairs of earth that was their issue. Of course, he had to admit that he did give mankind a little push now and then when they were standing on the edge of doom.

God looked with pity on this rebellious, former angel that He still loved, but this was lost on the lone figure who stood in front of Him. Years and eons ago, He could have extinguished Lucifer's life with the snap of His fingers, but He was hoping still to reach him before the end came. Lucifer, however, was just too defiant and preoccupied with his own interests to care anymore.

Gabriel stood silently nearby, eyeing the whole situation from enough of a distance to feel safe. Gabriel's ability to love was far more limited than the One they all stood before. Satan had always been a force on the playing field, whose dealings Gabriel had to counter and hold in check, on nearly an hour by hour and day by day basis. After years of watching the travels of this sinister figure, he could not shift his gaze away for a moment, even though he was in this heavenly assembly with the Lord nearby. It had just become habit. Being in charge of the force of angels that guarded the earth instead of harming it, he had been constantly vigilant to Satan's movements for as long as he could remember. But he looked forward to a day when this would not be so, a day where he could disband his forces and relax.

It was hard. The Lord alone knew when that day would be and Gabriel knew that He kept it to Himself. Waiting until then on a daily basis was difficult. God's love and patience was something Gabriel didn't understand, but he did trust this One he loved and served.

There was hushed silence in the assembly when the Lord finally spoke.

"Where have you been?" said God in a sure but commanding voice, opening up the conversation for all to hear. Though He already knew, He asked again, "Where have you come from?"

"Oh, from roaming throughout the earth, going back and forth in it," Satan answered the Lord vaguely, with a slight smile forming on his face. In this moment Satan couldn't successfully cover his hatred for everything that presently stood around him, though he tried to feign an air of innocence about his travels.

He thought for a moment of where he actually had been this morning and what he had been up to – just before his arrival. He thought no one actually knew, but that was naïve on his part. His 'roaming' had always been destructive and this was known to all in attendance – so this look of innocence he had was absurd. His movements about the earth on a daily basis were not benign, but more like that of a tiger or leopard in the zoo, pacing within a cage. Your safety depended on the seemingly small, thin bars of the cage between you and the tiger looking unendingly at you. As it paced it's only thought was getting out and getting to you, as you were simply prey to it. Such was the character of the personage before them.

Gabriel's eyes still remained riveted on Satan.

"Though business has been time consuming," Satan said with a smile, "I thought it might be of interest to you all that I have taken up some sports in my off time." He looked around so see if any found a sense of humor in this.

There was some low murmuring and some looks by those in the heavenly assembly. It was such an absurdity for him to mention time off and this whole dialogue of his was beginning to wear thin on the assembly. It was a poor joke for sure and no one laughed or moved. They looked away from Satan to the Lord to see His reaction.

The One before them all looked painfully again at this lone figure. The angels were wondering where this was going, but God knew all too well what Satan meant by the words he spoke. It was the angels that needed to hear him out, as there was something important that the Lord wanted His protectors of earth to understand.

"Go on," He said to Satan.

The Deceiver looked at the Lord, but out of the corner of his eye he knew that he had the full attention of his audience now too. Satan swelled with pride, as he craved this kind of attention.

"Yes, I have tried archery, golf, basketball, polo, football, cricket and many other sports," said the Oppressor of mankind, "and I found them interesting, but they were ultimately boring activities. Only one ball and one point at a time – just not enough action for my tastes. But I've finally found a game that is much more appealing to me . . . . it's bowling."

"I see," said the One before him, "Please continue as I'm sure this will be of interest to us all."

It was here that the formerly beautiful angel, who turned from a perfect life to a certain future of darkness and death, could control himself no longer. His voice took on a sneer, his very presence changed, and his anger began to truly emerge as he continued to speak. "Destroying one man or one woman at a time with an arrow or a club is fine, if you have plenty of time on your hands, but in the end it's *really a lot of work.* Yes, bowling is more my type of game."

The silence of those whose who stood near God continued as their eyes remained fixed on the Devil.

"What a joy it is to take out the head pins and leave a split; that's my favorite," he said, almost to himself. His glee began to turn into a chuckle.

"Yes, while you all have been *sleeping,* I've found out that with one ball I can get more action than just a game that gives me one point or one person at a time."

They began to understand that he wasn't talking about sports really at all.

"With the parents standing in front as head pins," he continued, "when I take them out I get all the rest behind them. Yes, the loss of them standing in front of the family, protecting together, is more than enough discouragement to affect the kids, grand-parents, supporting relatives, neighbors, and those living nearby in their communities. I can even wreak havoc on future generations to come. And it's amazing – I can't resist this last part – I've even gotten Your people to make excuses about all this and buy into the destruction as well, regardless of what You have told them."

It was especially quiet now.

"You know . . . . I like that kind of value for my efforts . . . yes sir, I do." He laughed uproariously and viciously, then he turned to leave. One last look at them all, and the lone figure slowly diminished from sight as he disappeared, still laughing, into the distance.

After he was gone, the Lord gathered the remaining faithful around Him.

"So you know now what you must now do," He said as He looked at them with intense seriousness. "I wanted you to know what he is up to, that's why I let him speak. Please," He said as He looked around Him to all of them one more time, "please pay extra attention to guarding the families, especially the husbands and wives – so much depends on it."

It was a quiet and sober assembly that disbanded that morning to pursue their tasks.

Marriage Conduct

'Get rid of all bitterness, rage, anger, harsh words, and slander, as well as all types of evil behavior. Instead, be kind to each other, tenderhearted, forgiving one another, just as God through Christ has forgiven you.'

Paul
Ephesians 4:25 – 32
New Living Translation

Marriage

I want to say up front that what you don't deal with in dating becomes a further assignment to deal with in marriage. Irritating or demoralizing issues are not going to evaporate in to thin air, and the whole thing isn't going to blow over like the sun coming out after a storm on the prairie. When issues don't get resolved in your marriage, because you don't want to rock the boat, then they may become burrs in your saddle that make you want to get off of the horse altogether. Don't come to that spot – deal with them. Be willing to listen to whatever your spouse has to say – without judgement or comment. If your spouse isn't listening, have an intercessory meeting with a few very close friends or plan out some harder steps.

Knowing what you know now, it would have been nice to have dealt with them earlier, while dating – but you didn't. Welcome to the human race. Just know that you don't get to skip a prerequisite class and still graduate from college. There is no click of the heels 3 times and your problems go away. I guarantee it will be more uncomfortable the longer you put off things that you need to deal with between you. So begin to deal with the issues now, one by one, patiently.

⌒

Marriage is such an essential thing to life, maybe the most. Why is that?

Outside of those vital parts of life taken care of by the Maker of our Universe, in marriage we expect to find the deepest needs of our being and our hearts being met.

- We are searching for someone who will set aside the rest of their lives for us, and we for them. This is faithfulness and commitment.
- We want someone who will get to know us better than anyone else will, hoping that after they do, they will still stay to love and care about us. We want to do the same for someone else. This is friendship, trust and forgiveness.
- We want someone that will sit beside us and hold our hands, touch our hair, stroke our skin, and look into our eyes. We want a hug of affection and the warmth of a touch when we come home. And when the opportunity presents itself, we want that deepest level of intimacy and physical acceptance that we can have. This is affection and passion.

Some say they can live without passion but I would be hesitant to try. To me it is the difference between sparkling cider and water, mom's anything and meals out of a box, a candle burning in place of one that is blown out, and the fragrance of a rose compared to the smell of a trash heap. It scares me to think of a life without it. Passion may transition a bit as time goes on, understandably, but if possible I want to be sitting across from the one I love at 90 and still have a tinge of emotion when I look at them. Our hearts, until they stop beating, need passion.

- We want someone who will miss us if we're not there, and we them. This is way more than just not wanting to be alone; it is a person that will be looking in earnest if we're late in arriving home, who would never be the same if we were gone from this life forever - the same way that we would feel about them. Though in a crowded room surrounded by many people or if we are miles away; even if we transverse the boundaries of this life, they will not stop thinking of us – daily, as the years go by. This is true oneness.

- We want someone with whom we can share what we think, without fear of total rejection. It's a mixture of trust, acceptance and respect for who we are. It wouldn't be unquestioned acceptance – as that isn't usually an acceptable position between 2 people. We would want the others feedback, combined with their opinions and insights, because we care about what they think also. That's one of the reasons we married them – we respected their wisdom and judgement. This is respect and intelligence.
- In short, we want to be as complete as possible. In an earthly sense, we want to be with someone we love and at rest in life when we are with them.

The hard part is that we're trying to get all these things from another human being – a person sitting across from us, who has their own needs also. It can turn into a tug-of-war at times. We hope they are willing or in the mood to give us what we need at the times we need it, but they hope for the same things to come from us also. They will have daily priorities to juggle like we do; obligations to meet and hard days at work to overcome – seemingly feeling alone. We thought it would just be receiving, but we must be there for them. We are called on to care for them too – maybe at an inconvenient time for us. When it's tough, or if we get neglected for too long, we may be tempted to strategize or plot ways to get them to give back to us. Maybe this is why it's critical to understand the needs of the person you're going to be with, to see if you're capable of giving them what they need.

Equally critical to the situation, with so much needing to be given between two people, is our maturity. Some of our wants are justified; however, on other issues, are we able to give back without always expecting to get something or anything immediately in return? Is there joy in just being with them?

This brings us to the One in life who never sleeps and is always there. Ideally, it is in marriage that we should come to understand our need for a personal relationship with God and how He can support us when no one else can – including our spouse. This priceless relationship with Him and the understanding that comes with it can help us meet our needs so we can meet the needs of the ones we love. They need Him too, of course. But with Him we are strong enough now, in this new way, to love the ones dear to us without constantly expecting an immediate return.

⌒

I want to put a few more things before you for your consideration.

Your marriage is important to others – so don't take that lightly

It is sobering when you understand the influence regular people and their marriages can have on their culture.

In a document about homosexuality and its effect on any nation or society, a hot button in Christian communities for sure, a group called The Ramsey Colloquium wrote about this subject in a way that might surprise you.

"We are not a 'representative group' of Americans, nor are we sure what such a group would look like. No group can encompass the maddening and heartening diversity of sex, race, class, cultural background, and ideological disposition that is to be found among the American people. . . . Our aim is to present arguments that are public in character and accessible to all reasonable persons. In doing so, we draw readily on the religious and moral traditions that have shaped our civilization and our own lives. We are confident that arguments based, inter alia, on religious conviction and insight cannot legitimately be excluded from public discourse in a democratic society.

While the gay and lesbian movement is indeed a new thing, its way was prepared by, and it is in a large part a logical extension of, what has been called the sexual revolution. The understanding of marriage and family once considered normative is very commonly dishonored in our society and, too frequently, in our communities of faith. Religious communities and leaderships have been, and in too many cases remain, deeply complicit in the demeaning of social norms essential to human flourishing. Thus, moral criticism of the homosexual world and movement is unbalanced, unfair and implausible if it is not, at the same time, a criticism of attitudes and behaviors that have debased heterosexual relations. The gay and lesbian insurgency has raised a sharp moral challenge to the hypocrisy and decadence of our culture. In the light of widespread changes in sexual mores, some homosexuals understandably protest that the sexual license extended to 'straights' cannot be denied to them . . .

Religious communities that have in recent decades winked at promiscuity [even among the clergy], that have solemnly repeated marriage vows that their own congregations do not take seriously, and that have failed to concern themselves with the devastating effects of divorce upon children, cannot with integrity condemn homosexual behavior unless they are also willing to reassert the heterosexual norm more believably and effectively in their pastoral care. In other words, those determined to resist the gay and lesbian movement must be equally concerned for the renewal of integrity, in teaching and practice, regarding traditional sexual ethics."

Did you catch all that? The homosexual movement, and the likes of it, is laid at the feet of folks *like you and I*. It is, they say, because we have abandoned our traditional beliefs that fringe groups have now appeared in greater numbers. In other words, we 'straights' have opened a larger door by our own immorality or by winking at these goings on in others that we know. Odd that our debasement doesn't bother us – but we are sure bothered by its collective reaction downstream. We need to face the evidence that we are at fault – maybe chiefly at fault like the Ramsey group declares. The value of marriage, and the values that make up marriage, are among those special things that are of the highest importance in His eyes. *But they are just as important for the eyes of human beings around us to see too.*

Dating properly is so important to a successful marriage

Having reviewed dating pretty thoroughly, I began to see how important it is to get to know someone, go through ups and downs, and to invest the proper amount of time during the dating process to see what the relationship would be like. Unfortunately that is too rare. I think a sizeable quantity of us get married on the high of being with this new person that is charming. The special feelings we have for this other person seem to intensify early on, so we feel it's love. We want this feeling we're having with this person for all time, so we go for it. We shorten the pre-relationship because we can't wait to get started. Maybe we also are afraid we'll lose them to someone else, so we take the leap rather than the loss, hoping we can work it all out.

Then you get in a marriage and really start to know each other – or you actually begin to understand the situation like you should have done before. The rosy picture begins to take a more realistic turn. Maybe it turns sour or maybe it just isn't the continual high. Either way, it can be disillusionment or a huge shock, depending on the circumstances.

I personally think you have to go through some steps to get to know someone thoroughly, and that you will either do this in dating or you will complete these steps you've missed in marriage. Depending on how drastic things are, you may have to complete them during a time of separation.

To go forward into marriage without the proper evaluation invites disaster. Some people complain that their partner turned out to be this or that and they never saw it coming. But could it be that we just didn't wait long enough to get to know them? I think so – or maybe we were too immature ourselves to see it.

Don't rush into marriage – enjoy the time together and trust the journey. If you're afraid they'll leave if you don't take them off the market then you really don't trust that it's love between you. It should be like a Billy Graham Crusade where it was always said that your friends will wait for you until you're done figuring out your life down front. I'm also not advocating that you dally around unnecessarily, but take the time you need to be sure. And if they leave because you're being careful - then let them leave. They would have probably left you at some point anyway.

So now you're married – what do you do? There is a remedy to all this; just admit to yourselves that you skipped certain steps and determine now to finish the things you should have covered ahead of time before. It's a little more difficult now that you're married, but get about the business of working it out and maturing together. If one doesn't want to participate, don't stop going after the issues of growth personally. At some point you may have put your foot down within your relationship if you don't see participation – but be patient at first. If you eventually have to take a stand, what kind of action you decide to take just depends on the issue - but stick it out. You can make it and you both can succeed.

Have faith in the future, especially when you get confused

I remember staring into a cup of coffee and not being able to say anything. When I lift my head, I can look around the room at the people sitting nearby, watching them converse back and forth about their lives together. But I'm sitting across from my loved one and there is a terrible silence between us. I think its times like this that you need to look ahead, into the future, and begin to change the direction of your lives. Start with confession if need be, but move the tiller toward a different heading and set the sails for better winds ahead.

You won't know it all when you get married, and at times it will get very confusing – beyond belief and description. I've been there. Emotions come and go, and life seems better in some other place, or you think it would be easier with someone else. You feel that you made a mistake and hope seems to just die within you at times. My admonition is to just tie a knot in it and hold on. Pray – as you probably needed to all along. Holding on sounds like desperation but it will be regarded as a talent later, one that was developed during these difficult times. Just wait until you get an answer that will bring you together in the long run, instead of panicking and taking a course that drives you apart.

I remember years ago that I heard that a friend had a motorcycle accident. He had gone for a ride and had gotten himself into a turn that seemed to be beyond his ability. With the bike leaned over, going faster than usual and the turn steadily getting sharper, his life went from a good day with confidence, to a bad day with sudden panic. I can see it all clearly, as though I was there. He had not gotten beyond the capabilities of the motorcycle, but he had gotten beyond his ability to know what to do. It seemed like there was nothing more he could do as the turned tightened, so he started to look for a place to land. He looked away from the corner to the outside of the road and off he went. From this difficult event (my friend survived and was OK) I got the important moral of the story - that where you look is where the bike is going to go. Most people who are professionals in motorsports know this truth or they wouldn't have survived. A rider needs to look away from trouble and keep his focus on the solution. It is not a natural decision for anyone to make; instead, it is a learned ability. Now that I ride motorcycles I am grateful for this second hand knowledge.

Marriage is this same issue. You're over your heads and you don't know what to do. I say have faith that there is a solution. Wait with a prayer for guidance and a resolve to be able to find it, and keep your focus on the importance of keeping your marriage together. Your situation can seem impossible, and help may not come as fast as you want it – I know. But others have found a way in similar circumstances. You may feel alone but you are not alone, nor the first ones to go through this kind of difficult water.

Dr. David Jeremiah gave a series on 2 Peter 1:3 – 11, dealing one by one with the topics therein of adding virtue, knowledge, self-control, endurance, godliness, brotherly kindness and love to our faith. He made a point on endurance that was especially meaningful to me. He said someone told him, "If you're going to quit, quit tomorrow. And when you get to tomorrow, put it off for another day."

So I give this to you for your consideration also - 'quit tomorrow.'

We will talk in a few moments about The Forgotten Option of taking a break if certain situations get too difficult for the both of you, but I first want you to see that you're not alone if your marriage is far from perfect. There are some people and some marriages that we have deemed as being ideal – but they are not. It doesn't mean they're bad either; you may just need to get a better perspective of what really goes on in any marriage.

Remember God's fictitious words to Adam and how true they are; "Son, you can't live with her and you can't live without her." There is balance and imbalance in any good relationship.

You may not know what to do at times and you may feel like quitting – but I ask you to never give up on your marriage. We need you more than you know. I know it's tough and you probably think you're insignificant, like it wouldn't matter if you blended into the woodwork or not. But you are a 'point of light', as one of our statesmen said. We need your marriage to make a difference – and it will. Our spouses, our kids, our neighborhoods, churches, and cities – even our nation and the world at large – will be a better place because of your commitment.

Hold fast.

CHAPTER **7**

Jesus On Marriage

Marriage

'Two are better off than one, for they can help each other succeed. If one person falls, the other will reach out to help. But someone who falls alone is in real trouble.

Likewise, two people lying close together can keep each other warm. But how can one be warm alone? A person standing alone can be attacked and defeated, but two can stand back-to-back and conquer.

Three are even better, for a triple-braided cord is not easily broken.'

Solomon
Ecclesiastes 4:9 – 12
New Living Translation [NLT]

Jesus's comments on marriage

So what does the greatest person who ever lived say about marriage?

It's interesting that He would say anything at all about this subject actually. A lot of great men and women have reached their status in the annals of history without having to talk about or deal with the subject of marriage, or maybe even defend their personal lives on this matter either. It says a lot about Him that He cared about this topic and spoke about it often. I have to warn you a bit that you would have probably been more cautious and accommodating on the subject than He, especially if it was your status you cared about protecting. But He puts the quest for popularity aside and takes a pretty narrow stance, for some, on what it means to be a man and a woman joined together for life.

There are those who are not religious and they just don't care what He said about anything – this is one end of the spectrum. On the other end there are those who take His words seriously, like they will be accountable to Him some day. I don't know what to think, but it is odd to me when someone says they are of the Christian faith but they want to numb, ignore, or silence His words on certain subjects. Is it because His statements make us feel uncomfortable? Is it because we just don't like what He says? I think of true character as being the ability to listen and digest things that are difficult, even if I don't agree. But instead, there are times I see strong reactions and evasive maneuvers among certain Christian people when someone allows Jesus to speak His mind.

This is especially true when the conversation turns to what Jesus said on marriage and divorce.

I guess I shouldn't be totally surprised actually. History records that the 12 disciples He handpicked choked more than a little when they heard His comments about what was His highest desire for this area of commitment between a man and his wife. They had to pull Him aside later and say in essence, "What! Do you really expect . . . !"[1]

For me, the difference between them and some today is that even though they had a hard time swallowing what He had to say, they still accepted it as part of His whole teaching. It stopped them in their tracks for sure and they initially cried 'impossible!', but they didn't seek thereafter to modify or dilute His meaning. They continued to follow Him in truth and spirit, even if they struggled in faith and in deed. I think this is an important thing to take note of. Even if we don't like His truths, at least hear them out and don't white wash it all when you're done. And if you quote Him, like we would anyone else, quote Him accurately.

I guess there are those who will always want the 'meek and mild' Jesus, with words and feelings that are more sublime. This person, who confidently and with impartiality strides through the pages of history, is sometimes too much for their sensibilities. "Oh, that we could have sat down with all of them back then," they might be saying to themselves, "so we could have touched this whole thing up a bit. We need to make these passages a bit more palatable for the world at large to consume. Maybe more people would come to Him if things were more reasonable. What we're seeing here is far too narrow."

Well maybe not. What would you be coming to that is life changing if you remove the truth?

In his book on the history of the Roman culture, Will Durant talks about the unfiltered honesty of the Apostles in regards to what they saw and heard. In his comments he said that they could have kept back some of the more questionable details – like Peter's denial or the moments of frustration with the disciples or the anguish that Jesus felt about His own fate that was to come – but they didn't. Instead of causing questions in people's minds it further cemented the authenticity of what they wrote about and described from first-hand knowledge.

I have a friend of mine who was converted to Christianity for this very reason mentioned by Durant. He was convinced of an unseen authority in the Bible because he felt the raw honesty of the text before him as he read. He felt sure that if this book had been written by men alone it would have been more sublime; it would have dealt with a whole lot of subjects in a much different manner. But it doesn't; it exposes human character in some extremely challenging and unflattering ways. For this very reason, my friend Keev discerned that he was in fact dealing with God speaking directly to him out of this book called the Bible. He felt that the God behind the Bible cared more for truth and reaching his soul, than whether it offended him in the process of doing so. I believe if we've been around the foundations of our faith for more than a few weeks, we should have already gotten used to the fact that we are dealing with a faith that will run crosswise to our 'sensibilities' on occasion. We don't control this figure in history nor will we silence Him. Many have tried.

What did Jesus say then about marriage that is so controversial to some?

Let's let Him speak for Himself.

"You have heard the law that says, 'A man can divorce his wife by merely giving her a written notice of divorce.' But I say that a man who divorces his wife, unless she has been unfaithful, causes her to commit adultery. Any anyone who marries a divorced woman also commits adultery."[3]

'Some Pharisees came and tried to trap Him with this question: "Should a man be allowed to divorce his wife for just any reason?"

"Haven't you read the scriptures?" Jesus replied. "They record that from the beginning 'God made them male and female.'" And He said, "This explains why a man leaves his father and mother and is joined to his wife, and the two are united into one. Since they are no longer two but one, let no one split apart what God has joined together."

"Then why did Moses say in the law that a man could give his wife a written notice of divorce and send her away?" they asked.

Jesus replied, "Moses permitted divorce only as a concession to your hard hearts, but it was not what God had originally intended. And I tell you this, whoever divorces his wife and marries someone else commits adultery – unless his wife has been unfaithful."

Jesus' disciples then said to him, "If this is the case, it is better not to marry!"

[I told you they choked – this is the spot].

"Not everyone can accept this statement," Jesus said, "only those whom God helps. Some are born as eunuchs, some have been made eunuchs by others, and some choose not to marry for the sake of the Kingdom of Heaven. Let anyone accept this who can."'[4]

⌒

'Then Jesus left Capernaum and went down to the region of Judea and into the area east of the Jordan River. Once again crowds gathered around Him, and as usual He was teaching them.

Some Pharisees came and tried to trap Him with this question: "Should a man be allowed to divorce his wife?"

Jesus answered them with a question: "What did Moses say in the law about divorce?"

"Well, he permitted it," they replied. "He said a man can give his wife a written notice of divorce and send her away."

But Jesus responded, "He wrote this commandment only as a concession to your hard hearts. But 'God made them male and female' from the beginning of creation. This explains why a man leaves his father and mother and is joined to his wife, and the two are united into one. Since they are no longer two but one, let no one split apart what God has joined together."

Later, when He was alone with His disciples in the house, they brought up the subject again. He told them, "Whoever divorces his wife and marries someone else commits adultery against her. And if a woman divorces her husband and marries someone else, she commits adultery."[5]

⤳

"Until John the Baptist, the Law of Moses and the messages of the prophets were your guides. But now the Good News of the Kingdom of God is preached, and everyone is eager to get in. But that doesn't mean that the law has lost its force. . . .

For example, a man who divorces his wife and marries someone else commits adultery. And anyone who marries a woman divorced from her husband commits adultery."[6]

⤳

So, there are some pretty plain thoughts I think we can see from the words that Jesus spoke on marriage and divorce.

I want to say upfront that I don't think you need someone to elaborate on all of this for you. You need to read these passages for yourself, maybe talk with your spouse or a good friend, until all of this becomes clearer to you. It might make more sense this way. Others are there to give you some help if you find the concepts fuzzy, but stretch yourself first by trying to understand what He is saying on your own. I think it's a good practice. I am not against outside commentaries by good authors either – I just think we should always try first to understand ourselves before we ask for someone else's opinion. Your convictions will only come from what *you believe.*

For me, if I had to summarize all of this in a short paragraph, I would say that He is clearly for marriages and asks that they last for a lifetime. So much is joined when a couple marries, but even more is destroyed, more than what was in the original joining, when they part. He gives a single reason here [sexual unfaithfulness] whereby a marriage can be dissolved, and He doesn't command that the dissolution take place for reasons of unfaithfulness – it's just an allowable concession where needed. For everything but this one reason, by reason of His silence, He says all else is workable.

We will talk about how things can be worked out, but if you're looking for another exclusion clause from Him it doesn't exist. There should be no confusion – the answer from silence is no. To Him I believe it is stronger than just betrayal or abandonment if someone leaves a marriage for good, going off to find someone else. I think He sees it as a ongoing, lifetime act of adultery. And it is not adultery against just your spouse, but it affects all others around us that we should care about too. In the end, it finally comes between us and Him.

And I will say again and again for emphasis, for the one who leaves there is generally one that wanted them to stay. A mutual agreement to part is truly very rare.

So if you've had a chance to go over what He said yourself, and you're willing to go a little further, let's look at it together and compare notes.

Notes

1. On marriage and divorce: The New Testament – Matthew, chapter 19:8-12 [NLT]
2. Caesar and Christ; A History of Roman Civilization and of Christianity from their beginnings to A.D. 325 [Simon and Schuster, New York: 1944]

3. On marriage and divorce: The New Testament – Matthew, chapter 5:31-32 [NLT]
4. On marriage and divorce: The New Testament – Matthew, chapter 19:3-12 [NLT]
5. On marriage and divorce: The New Testament – Mark, chapter 10:2-12 [NLT]
6. On marriage and divorce: The New Testament – Luke, chapter 16:16-18 [NLT]

What About Divorce?

"Can a man divorce his wife for any reason – giving her a written notice of divorce and send her away?"

In these times that Jesus lived I would imagine that it was more of a man's world. This question above is from a man, stated from a man's point of view. However, it doesn't mean that women didn't divorce then either, because remember that He also states in one of these sections,

"And if a woman divorces her husband and marries someone else, she commits adultery."[1]

People are people, so we know that this same condition and feeling existed within the hearts of women in that day also. And so it goes on – right on the same course today. What we will probably see as long as time exists are people of both sides and sexes not wanting, or willing, to live together any more in their original marriage commitment relationship. In our day it is interesting and personally confusing to me that at least 80% of the divorces today are initiated by women. This is a startling number from a group that I would have least expected it from.

Notice that this quote from the religious leaders of Jesus day is "Can I send the other spouse away?" – and not, "Should I send them away?" Basically, in this case, these men that are speaking are not asking, "What is the right thing for me to do?" Almost like a child who wants their way, they are saying, "I want to do this or that and have my own way – can you stop me?" No we can't, has been the answer down through the centuries. Some, like this line of questioning implies, aren't interested in whether it's right or wrong. It's not a point of reasoning or debate for them – so save your breath. They just want what they want – and in this case they want out. This reveals their heart and therefore this is where the main issue Jesus spoke about comes into play.

First of all, it is a heart issue and I suppose the heart issue should have been taken care of way back in the dating or courtship process – maybe even going back to one's family roots. Maybe we didn't date long enough to go through some hard times or tough spots together, to reveal where our hearts could be when things got tough. Maybe we needed to understand each other better before we got married, but were too much in love with love to wait. I don't think these are game enders. We are here in this relationship now, with our choice of someone we initially cared about and probably way down deep still do. We can make it work. I think we need to make it work.

Know that a hard heart isn't a good thing to have ever. It seems to be an attitude that one takes in anger against choice that they themselves made. It is not really about their spouse but it is really more of a closer look at them and their behavior over their own decisions. They evidently have had some wavering going on – and now, in their selfishness they want a 'mulligan' so they can take a different course. They have hardened their own heart by their own choice, thinking it is a better for them to go a different way rather than to meet their obligations. Maybe this is in part why second marriages have such a poorer chance of success than the originals; one's character never had a chance to properly develop in the original situation where it needed to. As my parents used to say, the grass is not greener on the other side.

⌇

When I think of my generation, 'the boomers', I remember that we were going to do things better than our parents who came before us. We were more gifted by insights and less burdened by tradition. We were going to show them how life was meant to be lived when one was given the freedom to shuck the old boundaries. But as I see it, this wasn't how it turned out. My parent's generation loved out of a sense of duty when things got tough. They dwelt on the good times they had together when going through the tough moments. They believed in sticking it out for the sake of the kids and had faith that the sun would come out from behind the clouds eventually. A lot of us 'boomers' laughed at all that, but they were eventually proved right in my opinion. I think my generation has let this current generation down far more than my parents would have done, if they had of been in our place.

Lastly, for those who have a religious sense, we need to see ourselves. We should care what God thinks about anything and everything – and why He feels this way. We need to explore what He's thinking in greater depth so we can make better decisions going forward. And in the larger scope of things, we should have a major change of heart regarding these things He asks us to obey. If not, what is our faith about? Are we just in a social circle or is something meaningful happening in our midst?

I don't believe that the scriptures teach that you can have the heart change you need without spending time at God's feet, hearing His words through reading the Bible, listening to what He has to say. The trends we see in the churches of today I believe are centered around this one issue – not spending quality time alone with God by myself, and you by yourself.

I personally spent years taking my family to church, punching the clock and putting in the time, thinking that we were growing together in the faith by our attendance. I came to realize many years later, when I see now that none of them have continued to follow, that there was something we had missed. I found it first in myself – my personal relationship with Jesus was a mess. I truly had the new birth and I could trust that He indeed was my Savior, but I didn't know what it was really like to talk to Him. If you had put me in a room alone and told me to come out after I had spent some time with Him, I wouldn't have known what to do. I'd probably still be in that room today. I didn't spend daily time with Him on a regular basis, or read the Bible enough to hear His voice and better understand what He desires. And so my poor attitude and lack of relationship took root in the family that I was raising. We didn't spend time together like we should have as a family first of all, and we sure didn't spend time during the week talking about anything God related. My wife begged me to have regular dinner times together as a family, but I was too stupid and self-absorbed to hear it. I regret all of this.

Regardless of all my church attendance, communion, giving, teaching, solemn observances and church activities of those days, I didn't love my family as I should have and I didn't do the Christian basics. I should have been a better man and a better father. God forgive me - and hopefully I can turn this around as much as possible.

I know now that we really don't have to wait till heaven to spend time with Him. In just the same way our eternal life begins here when we accept His offering of forgiveness, so also does the open door to speak with Him begin here too. Our relationship with Him doesn't need to wait until 'someday'; we can start now.

I hope our times with Him will include our family and especially our spouses – wife or husband. This is the essence of the Christian life – the quality of our relationships with Him measured by the effect that it can have on your family – and eventually, to others beyond that circle.

Notes

1. A woman divorcing a man: The New Testament – Mark, chapter 10:12 [NLT]

Is It Legal?

"What does the law say?"

For society to operate correctly it needs to provide guidance to its citizens in the right ways to live, and also allow for consequences for those who will follow their own ways. It is an 'if you do' and 'if you don't' situation. What are the legal laws of the nation in which you personally live? Right or wrong, what boundaries are you supposed to live within as a citizen of your community or country?

Sometimes laws can be wrong, but not often in my personal experience. For most of my life in America, if a law was passed you could generally believe it was for your own good and thereby trust it. But sometimes laws are not right. It may be a sidetrack, but such is my feeling about the legalization of marijuana in our day, found in several of our united states.

I was corrected by some younger people involved in this industry when I called it marijuana. "It's *cannabis*," they said. Would you mind telling me what the difference is? Someone's being deceptive when they take the garbage, wrap it in a different package, and call it roses. And this marijuana ['cannabis'] is far more potent than the stuff of my day[1]. I can't help but feel anger when adults pass laws without regard for morality or society; laws which their children will inherit to their own detriment. We seem to be saying in this instance, "This is OK – come on, do this." To the generation following our heel prints, it will not be a good way to go. This saddens me and I fear the repercussions, both now and for the days that follow.

So, if I meet the standards of right and wrong in regard to my present culture, it should be fairly evident that I won't always be doing the right thing. Realize that just asking 'What does the law say?' is not a *spiritual* question. If someone you know starts with only the letter of the law and ends with this same approach, the chances are they are not a moral or spiritually minded person. There is a morality at work that becomes the basis of the law, but often it gets diluted in most cases to just the basics. If I was a truly a moral, spiritually minded person, the law should only remind me of my duties but not have to define what my responsibilities are.

Jesus' statement in regard to "What does the law say?" is only a stepping stone for what is to follow next. And that stepping stone in our day says that a smart and truly civil society recognizes that beyond the basics a Higher Law is always in play.

Notes

1. Suggested reading: Marijuana, Mental Illness, and Violence – address given by Alex Berenson at Hillsdale College. Imprimis – Hillsdale College / Alex Berenson – Author of 'Tell Your Children: The Truth About Marijuana, Mental Illness, and Violence.'

What Does the Bible Say About It?

"Haven't you read the Scriptures?"

"Haven't you read the Scriptures?" was a question He asked of those before Him. He knew the Scriptures well, but He wanted to know if those before Him knew what the Bible said regarding what they were speaking of. Since they weren't considering its principles or its influence, it was left to Him alone to remind them to think about what God might be saying about this topic before them. It is my belief that it shouldn't be just Jesus alone asking this question, but we should be asking ourselves this question as well. What would be wrong with our wanting to enquire of the Bible?

I hope we can see, especially today, that society cannot be a 'god' unto itself. This leads to despotism for all and domination by a few. The concept of being accountable to higher principles goes back to the roots of our nation and far beyond that. Any leading and successful society will always want to know what the truth is. It will guide them like a star, even if the principles it advocates are currently unattainable for them. Although Thomas Jefferson believed that human goodness and the collective reasoning of the people would always lead to right actions, few others did. John Adams believed in principle before people; and that in spite of the popular vote there were certain truths that should always prevail in the face of public opinion. Maybe it came from Adam's years of being a lawyer or common sense, but I agree.

President Washington echoed the same sentiments. In the words of his almost prophetical fare-well address, George Washington said,[1]

"Of all the dispositions and habits which lead to political prosperity, religion and morality are indispensable supports. In vain would that man claim the tribute or patriotism, who should labor to subvert these great pillars of human happiness, these firmest props of the duties of men and citizens. The mere politician, equally with the pious man, ought to respect and to cherish them. . . . **And let us with caution indulge the supposition that morality can be maintained without religion**. Whatever may be conceded to the influence of refined education on minds of peculiar structure, reason and experience both forbid us to expect that national morality can prevail in exclusion of religious principle."

The best of history bears this out and would tell us the same, if we will but listen. There are higher concepts than ours that need to be followed for our safety, security, morality and sanity.

So I would encourage all, regardless of our persuasions, be it religious or atheistic, it would do all of humanity good to ask themselves what does the Bible say about this thing that I'm doing, or this stance I've taken, or that which I believe in? Remember these are God's laws and principles at work, whether you or I believe in them or not. And like the major figure that Jesus is in this world, without argument or denial, the same is true of the Holy Scriptures that bear His name and His words. The Bible, Old and New Testament, will remain the greatest selling book of all time. It is interesting that you won't find it on the New York Times 10 best sellers list because it is a given – year after year.

Because today we can grab one off of any shelf, we usually forget that great people have died or suffered throughout the centuries to make sure we could have a version, on our shelf, in our own language. Cultures have been changed in very good ways through having a translation of the Bible in their own language.

I don't think that you'll hear this about any other book – especially those in the elite minority of works that have survived so long in human history as the Bible has. It seems that most of these aren't even relevant any more.

But this one work is. I recommend you take this book and consider what it says in a serious, thoughtful way. You will certainly better understand yourself by understanding its contents, for its principles lay there, waiting to educate you and I and be beneficial towards us.

As the world's best-selling book maybe all mankind won't read its contents as they should – as disappointing as that sounds. However, if they ask you or I, I hope that we will have an answer as to what it says about the situation that lays before us.

Notes

1. Washington's Farewell Address – 1796

Marriage

"My most brilliant achievement was my ability to be able to persuade my wife to marry me."

Winston Churchill

A Necessary Detour

When we talk about male, female and creation – which we will do in a bit – we find ourselves in the midst of origins and beginnings. I don't want to get too distracted while pursuing our subject of Jesus' feelings about marriage, but there are a few points I'd like to address that are important to our staying on track. I think it's proper to say something here about origins, for there are too many of us who will detach in the chapters ahead because the Biblical story of creation will seem too ludicrous. I understand this as very real possibility, so if you're not opposed to discussing origins, then please bear with me for the next few moments.

It was a major hurdle in my life to read 'Origin of Species by Means of Natural Selection' because I thought it would blow away all of my feelings about God and creation forever. But there came a point where it seemed inescapable to intellectually sidestep this whole issue – so I jumped in the deep end of the pool so to speak and began to study this book. Who better to read about evolution than Charles Darwin himself? I got my own copy of 'Origin of Species By Means of Natural Selection – or the Preservation of Favored Races in the Struggle for Life' and proceeded to review his work from beginning to end. What I found in the end was that I actually didn't lose my faith. To the contrary, it was such a rewarding pursuit that the impact of his work continues to have a profound influence on my life. I am further more amazed that so many have staunch views on evolution but have never picked up his book and have no idea of what he wrote.

I will try to be brief, but there are several issues Darwin raised that were of special importance to me.

⤚

The first thing I found was that Darwin determined that he needed a Creator for his theory to exist. It didn't change the fact that he believed in evolution, but he was wise enough in my opinion to know that something couldn't come from nothing. What this means is he needed God at the beginning of the equation, but he still felt that evolution could handle the ongoing development of all the existing species through the process of natural selection. But the concept of a beginning in his mind required a Creator to make any sense, and many times in his book he referenced this.

'It is scarcely possible to avoid comparing the eye with a telescope. We know that this instrument has been perfected by the long-continued efforts of the highest human intellects; and we naturally infer that the eye has been formed by a somewhat analogous process. But may not this inference be presumptuous? Have we any right to assume *that the* **Creator** works by intellectual powers like those of man?'[1]

'Let this process go on for millions of years; and during each year on millions of individuals of many kinds; and may we not believe that a living optical instrument might thus be formed as superior to one of glass, as the works *of the* **Creator** are to those of man?'[1]

'I see no good reasons why the views given in this volume should shock the religious feelings of any one ....

A celebrated author and divine has written to me that "he has gradually learned to see that it is just as noble a conception of the *Deity* to believe that **He created** a few original forms capable of self-development into other and needful forms, as to believe that *He* required a fresh act of creation to supply the voids caused by the action of *His* laws."'[2]

In this regard, what is most interesting to me is that in all the copies, from almost the very beginning in 1859 until about 2010, the following statement makes up the last paragraph of his work in 'Origins of Species.' I write this below from my own copy which goes back to 1959.

'Thus, from the war of nature, from famine and death, the most exalted object which we are capable of conceiving, namely, the production of the higher animals directly follows. There is a grandeur in this view of life, with its several powers, *having been originally breathed by the* **Creator** *into a few forms or into one*; and that, *while this planet as gone circling on according to the fixed law of gravity*, from so simple a beginning endless forms most beautiful and most wonderful have been, and are being evolved.'[2]

Why is it that this statement has since been modified in the newer versions, with the word 'Creator' removed? We won't have time to look at this, but you should think about this for yourself. The prior references of his that I give, the words 'having been originally breathed' in the paragraph above, remain – until they are possibly removed also. These give direct reference to a Creator and tie into Genesis where God 'breathes life' into being.

The farthest Darwin wanted to go with his theory was the evolution of life on earth; remember his book is called the 'Origin of Species', not the 'Origin of the Universe and All Points In Between'. These concepts have been truly inserted by others. He knew, as we should, that he needed a universe, a planet circling in perfect orbit, sun light, water and all the elements we see on hand for life to exist and to evolve. He even mentions a 'fixed law of gravity' and a 'spinning planet' in his statement above as part of his foundational basis for evolution. But you can see pretty quickly that if you pull God out, as some have done, you now will have to figure out how to bring a universe to being and make matter come out of nowhere. Is this science – or have some entered into the realm of speculation and high fantasy?

When scientists of his day wanted to leave his theory of gradual evolution, requiring long eons of time to even be possible, and come up with their stories about sudden, miraculous evolution of a species that gave an animal something like wings over-night, Darwin said:

> 'He who believes that some ancient form was transformed suddenly through an internal force or tendency into, for instance, one furnished with wings, . . . he will further be compelled to believe that many structures beautifully adapted to all the other parts of the same creature and to the surrounding conditions, have been suddenly produced; and of such complex and wonderful co-adaptions, he will not be able to assign a shadow of an explanation. . . . To admit all this is, as it seems to me, to enter into the realms of miracle, and to leave those of science.'[3]

Such is the concept and those like it, of bringing a fire ball out of nowhere and thinking it will 'big bang' all that we see, living and non-living, into existence. This is to leave the realm of science and likewise enter into miracles. Take a tennis ball, or a hot rock, and blow it up in your driveway. Let me know if you come up with the creation of life or spinning planets hanging in the air before you. Realize that Darwin never had anything like this in mind.

My brother has his favorite saying that he reminds of me time and time again; and that is, *"not to start an argument in the middle of a sentence."* People from all walks of life can debate all the questions and topics on evolution found in the middle of the story line – but they are uncomfortable with talking about, "But where did it all come from?" I think this discussion of ultimate beginnings inescapably leads us back to either a belief in eternal matter, which somehow brought everything miraculously into being, or a Creator. Regardless of how uncomfortable it is for many, it is where we all need to begin. A proper look at beginnings will have a drastic effect on where we end up.

⌒

Secondly, there are deep problems with the concept of evolution. As much as Darwin tried to explain them away, at least I give him a nod for seeing them. Any true student of evolution, along with the casual observer, ought to acknowledge this – although the latter are not held as accountable for being well read on this subject. It's the former that call themselves experts that are the most frustrating to me personally, as they should know better; but how rarely I have dialogued with anyone who has conceded these issues, much less even read the material.

Darwin has more than one chapter dealing with contradicting issues he faced – like:

-   The vast inadequacy of the fossil record to show transitionary forms.

- How could evolution over time could evolve organs of extreme perfection?
- How did such amazing instincts get developed and then inherited by the next generation in ways we cannot even see?
- Why are there beautiful colors that would be obviously detrimental to a species survival, yet they exist in everything around us?
- We talk about evolution, but why do we not see it happening before our eyes – like half dog, half cats walking around?
- And more . . . . .

In regards to all this, he says in part:

'To arrive, however, at a just conclusion regarding the formation of the eye, with all its marvelous yet not absolutely perfect characters, it is indispensable that the reason should conquer the imagination; but I have felt the difficulty far too keenly to be surprised at others hesitating to extend the principle of natural selection to so startling a length.'[1]

'That many and serious objections may be advanced against the theory of descent with modification through variation and natural selection, I do not deny. I have endeavored to give them their full force. Nothing at first can appear more difficult to believe than that the more complex organs and instincts have been perfected, not by means superior to, though analogous with, human reason, but by the accumulation of innumerable slight variations, each good for the individual possessor.'[2]

I think it is very important to note as we examine his work, that about 80% of the science we have today has been developed since his time. All these things he conjectured, as simple as he thought they were, we are now finding them to be incredibly complex. I had a manager once that said the 'devil is in the details'. I think he was wrong. I think the deeper we dig we are finding that God is in the details, especially as we look at life. The universe and world we live in is like finding an Apple computer in an empty parking lot that is plugged in and working. We came into the world with all this in operation, and because of this we've often never developed a proper sense of wonder. To dispute or rationalize away the design and intricacy we see in DNA, molecular structures, chemistry, atomic energy, how organs of the body function, interact and are completely dependent on each other – to not see the amazing complexities of these things - is not to see. The questions Darwin posed in the past against his theory are evermore stronger today, to an exponential level, and cannot be ignored by a reasonable society.

⤿

I could go on, but I will give one more final consideration to think of.

One of the main reasons that this debate over origins, evolution or creation, gets so heated is because people don't realize that *it is a matter of faith*. At the end of the day it is your faith or mine, regardless of which side we take or how we look at it.

I can hear someone saying, if they're actually thinking at this point, "Now you've really ticked me off . . . . making such a ridiculous statement as this. I believe in science, but your creation story is a matter of faith – not mine. I only believe in the facts."

The reality of our combined situation, yours and mine, is that *we weren't there* when this whole issue of our origins was taking place – *no one alive today was there*. It wasn't on tape, nor was it videoed. The true definition of science is that it is something proven, that can be repeated over and over again. The origin of the universe however was a onetime event. It is therefore true, to some extent, that we are a bit stuck in the middle of the sentence so to speak when it comes to origins. The only thing we have is the ability to look at the evidence that was left to us in an unbiased way, as much as possible, to determine for ourselves which viewpoint makes the most sense. In the end it will be a matter of faith however, for no matter how scientific you claim be, no one alive was there for this one time event. Just have the best data possible is my admonition, from reliable sources, when you make your final conclusion.

Darwin spoke of this – our reviewing the data – and he hoped that we would have the courage to look at these issues soberly and factually, without a bunch of conjecture or over-emotional infusion. He wrote in 'Origins',

> 'A few naturalists, endowed with much flexibility of mind, and who have already begun to doubt the immutability of species, may be influenced by this volume; but I look with confidence to the future, to young and rising naturalists, **who will be able to view both sides of the question with impartiality.**'[2]

⤶

Speaking only for myself, after a lot of study, it remains a greater miracle for me to believe in what some call the evolutionary origins of life, than to just recognize that this complex system of life and genetics around us has a divine origin. I don't see it as a more believable viewpoint to think that life and matter has been brought about just by itself.

What I do see is the mention of distinct species, referenced in Genesis, when it says God brought created things forth to reproduce 'after their own kind.' I don't see any evidence of evolution going on around me, and what some tout as 'evolution' is better defined as variation among species, showing in reality their adaptability. I see huge gaps in the fossil record where millions of mutations should exist, and sedimentary layers where there should be erosion and truncation among the layers if millions of years transpired. I keep thinking of when I read, as a kid, that Richard Leaky was looking for the 'missing link' in Africa I believe. How absurd to mention 'a link' and not realize that it wouldn't be just one link but a millions of links that one would easily expect to find; actually of necessity, would have to find. And among many other things I could mention, I see the greatest Person in history believing the story of Genesis just like it was recorded and taught. I am not blindly following Him, as I have done my own research, but knowing what He believed just further caps the issue for me.

This sums it up as to where I stand – and you have your own decision to make. My admonition is to be sure your facts *are facts*. As Paul cautioned Timothy in one of his New Testament letters,

> 'O Timothy, keep that which is committed to your trust, avoiding profane and vain babblings, **and oppositions of science falsely so called:**'[4]

My last reference is to the book of Hebrews where it says,

> 'By faith we understand that the entire universe was formed by God's command, **that what we see now did not come from anything that can be seen.**'[4]

I hope this helps. Let's go back to marriage.

Notes

1. Origin of Species By Means Of Natural Selection; Or the Preservation of Favored Races In the Struggle For Life. Charles Darwin, M.A., F.R.S. Chapter VI – Difficulties of the Theory, Organs of Extreme Perfection.

2. Origin of Species / Charles Darwin: Chapter XV – Recapitulation and Conclusion

3. Origin of Species / Charles Darwin: Chapter VII – Miscellaneous Objections to the Theory of Natural Selection

4. Science falsely so called: The New Testament, 1 Timothy, chapter 6:20 [King James Version – KJV]

5. The universe not made from things we see: The New Testament – Hebrews, chapter 11:3 [NLT]

Male and Female They Stand

"God made them male and female from the beginning of creation."

It is interesting to me that the greatest historical figure that ever lived believed in creation, just as it was depicted in the writings of the Bible. Jesus believed in the account of the world starting with God making Adam and Eve, and He spoke of it often.

The statement He made of 'God made them male and female from the beginning' refers to the fact that 'male' and 'female' are a design that was made and meant to be joined together. You can see from the physical aspect of nature, and from the social and emotional make-up of men and women, that they were naturally meant to complement one another. I believe to deny this is absurd. The very core of nature and life around us screams this truth from the treetops.

There is also the purpose of the family that comes out of this design. It is the ability of a man and a woman to have children together and care for them, from start to finish, in an exemplary, protected environment that constitutes the family.

"This explains why a man leaves his father and mother and is joined to his wife, and the two are united into one."

The power of attraction coming from another person, then being drawn together and joined in a relationship is the catalyst for

163

wanting to ultimately be one in marriage together. It is an amazing thing to see love at work.

Solomon said,

> 'There are three things that amaze me – no, four things that I don't understand; how an eagle glides though the sky, how a snake slithers on a rock, how a ship navigates the ocean, and how a man loves a woman.'[1]

Something amazing also happens when two people become one that most aren't aware of. C.S. Lewis[2], using the skewed theology of the demons in the Screwtape Letters refers to how the man they called Paul believed that sex, whether married or not, sets up a bond between two people forever. It's the process, whether a couple is happy or unhappy, that automatically takes place to begin to make them one. In the play fast society that apparently surrounds us, I'm not sure people understand this truth.

Outside of the Bible, this relationship of 'oneness', or bonding isn't seen as clearly as it should be. If oneness is recognized, it is possibly seen as a partnership, a friendship, a 50/50 agreement or possibly a love relationship that one hopes will last.

The Bible however relates to us a different, far deeper story. It speaks of the spiritual and physical union between a woman and a man as being like glue or a magnet.

In the aspect of *glue*, once a marriage takes place this bond that is created between that man and that woman will remain forever. It doesn't matter whether one or both remain faithful to their relationship or not, the bond remains. This is what the glue was created to do. The torn garment or split wood joint will retain pieces of the original fabric even after being broken apart. This is the same with the ending of a marriage. We can see the torn remnants in people's lives just in our observations of broken relationships.

In terms of a *magnet*, the needle of the compass within us will always point toward that original union. That first decision will define the rest of our lives. This is why most separated people will feel uncomfortable around their former spouse, regardless of the time that has past. That internal magnet within each of them still recognizes the original marriage, the union they agreed to, and the needle swings this direction whenever they are around each other. The compass will remind them, for a lifetime, of the place they were both meant to be in.

There is also found here, in the statement Jesus made at the beginning of this chapter, the point of a person leaving a family and creating another family. This is a poignant statement that underlines the truth that one has a model of a marriage relationship, coming from their point of origin, as the only blueprint they have. It almost guarantees that they'll do the same unless some major changes are made. It will be difficult to blaze a new trail – but it can be done.

I have recognized how some have an advantage that they aren't even usually aware of when they have been raised in a home with the same original parents. I was going to say 'faithful, loving' parents as a caveat, but may I be so bold to say that if your parents stayed together, even if it was anything but perfect, you still have an advantage over others whose parents split apart during tough times. If your parents' marriage was great – then great! I say the largest part is that your parents modeled staying together for you. Adult children raised in this environment have unknowingly gone to 'Marriage University' growing up and were seated up front when the lessons were given out. They have been given the answers to the test before they took it, and they usually know what is expected of them in in their marriages because they have seen it modeled in their dad and mom's relationship when they were at home. Even if it wasn't a 'perfect' marriage they witnessed, they still had the same mom and dad to come home to; without court battles, split times of custody during the week, late nights all alone unsupervised, the mystery of trying to decide who was right and who was wrong, a 'new' mom or a 'new' dad to get used to and the constant pain of what you missed growing up. I'd rather have the 'poor' example of two parents that stuck it out than the infinitely poor example of two who quit.

Oh, what an advantage it is to have grown up seeing things as they should be! But oh, what a disservice we have done by destroying our own marriages and then expecting our children to succeed in their own! How ludicrous it is for any parent to think, "I've done my job by raising them and now they are on their own. What I do from this point won't matter. I'm free to pursue whatever I want for myself because it won't affect them; they're adults now." Remember that you are an example until the day you die.

I remember studying when I was a kid. I grew up in my home and found homework difficult to do. I didn't expect my parents to study with me or for me; I knew it was mine to do but it would have been nice to have their input. What was difficult for me about studying was to be in my room and hear them listening, in the background, to a favorite TV program in the living room. I was so distracted by this that I would put my studies down at times and just sit by the door of my room, with it slightly open, so I could listen also. My parents didn't study or read much in their private time, so I began to wonder what the use was of school work if the whole point of being an adult was to watch TV. I knew I wasn't supposed to skip an education, I just didn't have a strong example at home of how it was supposed to be done. It would have been easier in those years if they had been an example of something other than sitting on a couch watching TV in the evenings.

In an amazing book called 'The Unforeseen Legacy of Divorce'[3] the authors relate how children from highly dysfunctional, divorced families turned out against the background of those who were under the same circumstances but stuck together. The book related that there were equally troubling circumstances that both family examples suffered; the only difference was that one family stuck it out together and the other one didn't. In both cases these were families where you would have thought it best if the parents were separated forever and the children given to the CPA or put in foster homes. Again, the common denominator was one family stayed together (against all odds) and the other disbanded. (For the record, the authors would never advocate being in a violent, physically lethal environment. However, these were still situations where things had gone bad.)

All of us would naturally think that a family split apart under circumstances like these would have been saved from terrible memories and the daily exposure to the poor situation before them. But this is an adult perspective; the children still needed the security of their parents, regardless of how bad the situation was. It was sad that the adult children coming from the disbanded family had all the dysfunctional issues that the other family had, but had the further burden of seeing their parents split up. The extended families created from this situation had a lot of the same major issues, as well as marriages that didn't last. For the families that stayed together (against all odds) it was found that the adult children coming from this setting actually did quite well in their subsequent marriages and extended families. How is this possible? Surprisingly, it was the attitude these children took into their marriages from their parents staying together. They thought, "If mom and dad could stick it out, with all the problems and issues they had, then it will be a piece of cake for us."

Know that you are an example, for good or bad, until the day you leave this earth. I believe it is wise to live out your life to the highest standards you can, especially for the sake of your children, who will have to watch the way you live regardless.

Live life in the best way possible if you expect your children to do the same.

Notes

1. Things that are amazing: The Old Testament – Proverbs, chapter 30:18-19, [NLT]
2. The Screwtape Letters, chapter 18. C.S. Lewis / HarperCollins Publishers
3. The Unexpected Legacy of Divorce – A 25 Year Landmark Study: Introduction, page xxii – xv. Authors Judith Wallerstein, Julia Lewis and Sandra Blakeslee – Hyperion Publishing, Copyright 2000

When Did I Commit Adultery?

He told them, "Whoever divorces his wife and marries someone else commits adultery against her. And if a woman divorces her husband and marries someone else, she commits adultery."

When we think of adultery, we can say in its most basic terms that it is a married person being somewhere with someone they shouldn't be with. They are with another man or woman when they should be home, side by side, with their original partner.

I believe that most of us in general struggle when we see a couple and their marriage split-up. It is a hurtful situation – not just for them but for us too. Later, at the store or just in passing, to see one of the partners with someone else when the original spouse is alive and still affected, continues to not feel right - no matter how long it has been. We don't have to be closely involved like the children are or be an immediate part of the family to feel the hurt. If we were close enough to them to be friends or neighbors, or maybe spent years being around them at church or at work – the situation feels awkward no matter how long it's been. You miss the memories and the days when you spent time together when their original spouse was in the picture. You can't talk about those days, or the other person, when you are with them because they are now with someone else, who is possibly standing beside them when you are talking. I have felt this way around folks way too many times and I am sure I am not alone.

I believe that on the cross, what might have given Jesus the most agony was having to see all that mankind had done and was going to do. He was going to die for the world's offenses, and I believe He had to know intimately, probably in perfect detail, all that He was going to have to absorb as He gave His life for all of our sins, for all time. When it comes to this, I don't know how anyone could have seen all that he saw, in that moment of time, and be able to endure or handle it. This just would have been too much for any of us, but God, to endure.

Imagine being Him and having to look down upon earth, seeing all of the good and bad going on at once. Imagine as you're looking at the world and all of its people, you see Bob and Susan that used to be together. You remember that they used to be like candle light, shining together as one. But now He sees they are two distant lights far apart from each other on the earth below. You hear the prayers of those whose hearts were hurt due to this situation, you see the trouble ahead for the kids or one of the spouses, you see the intimacy and carefree life of one while the other suffers, and you see what could have been a wonderful life now broken into a thousand pieces. Sure, you're not going to like this any more than most humans do – but as God you will have to see this with greater clarity, and know ahead of time all of the damage that will be done. And you will be called on in prayer repeatedly to fix all of this because you are God. This isn't fun for Him to deal with.

This to me is why He wants to see all of us remain with our original partner – through the thick of it. Our lives are literally what He has to look at every day. And because He sees and knows all, I am certain He would like to look down on a world where relationships were worked out, lives were changed and where families stayed together for reasons of care and protection. Because of all this and more, this is why He regards divorce to be unfaithfulness too, when the world at large considers a second partner to just be another option.

We error when we think of adultery as just a fling outside of an existing marriage. Jesus shows here that He sees many, many second marriages as the same issue. Being married a second time is not wrong under certain conditions – namely the death of a previous spouse or the unchangeable unfaithfulness of a marriage partner. But so often these conditions are not the causes for the divorces we see. We find folks walking away when the original marriage could have been saved if all would have been patient, if someone would have waited for growth in one or the other, or if both learned that the end wasn't really the end but could have been worked out. The common denominator when looking down from above is seeing the original couple separated and two new people that shouldn't be together, whether outside of an existing marriage or within a second one. Whether it has been a one night fling, several months together, or 45 years of a faithful second marriage, it doesn't matter when one or both of them should have been home all these years with their original spouse.

I have a friend that grew up in a very nice home up until about the age of 7 – then everything fell apart. He had a working father who held a nice executive position at a large company, but he started an affair with a worker on the production floor that was eventually found out. Overnight, life for my friend changed dramatically. His dad lost his job because the affair but continued to see the woman and eventually married her. His mom found herself betrayed in the situation and was divorced by his father. As a result of all this his mom went from a big house to a small mobile home in a trailer park in short order. He saw his mom suffer when he was a boy and it continued on as he became a man. He had to help her to make financial ends meet through all of it. Eventually, probably out of desperation, his mom got married again but the man was an alcoholic and her life continued to spiral down and out of control until her death later on in life.

Years later my friend was taking his dad and his second wife to the airport. With his dad beside him and his wife in the backseat, she began to say, "Honey, we have had such a wonderful 40 years together – it has really been great." In that moment, I think my friend saw his growing up years and the destruction of their family in an instant. He looked at his father beside him and then looked at her in the rearview mirror and said, "It has been great . . for who? You both destroyed our family, hurt my mom and caused problems for all of us that remain with us to this very day. I'm glad it was great for you - but it wasn't great for the rest of us."

I don't know if things got quiet in the car or what happened after that, because I wasn't riding along. All I know is that he was right. This is a perfect illustration, showing that the number of years put into a second marriage still doesn't make it right. What starts off wrong and continues in the same wrong direction, remains wrong – regardless of the number of years that have passed or the events that have taken place in the meantime.

Peter Marshall, prior Chaplin to the US Senate, talks about growing up in the small Scottish town of his birth, and how if you lost something it was generally returned to you. There would be a posting in the paper the following day or during that week that would say something like;

Found: A small emerald ring . . . . . a wallet left on the seat of the morning bus . . . earring found on the corner of 4th and Ash . . . .'

I personally left my wallet once in our apartment laundromat: a neighbor found it and brought it back to me. It is a wonderful thing to have something lost returned to you.

It is the same with troubled marriages today where people lose their way. Just because someone left their spouse doesn't mean that they're *free to be taken*. Just because a couple is having a severe argument doesn't mean any of us have the right to move into their territory. To you they may not be coming back together, and you think you can see in his or her eyes that it's all over. You believe you're certain, by the way they walk or talk, that they are going to find someone else, *but it still doesn't have to be you*. How do you know, without talking to his or her previous spouse, what the real story is?

In the book bearing his name, Hosea the prophet gives an interesting perspective that I consider valid. The principle he gives centers on a real life event that involved himself, a woman named Gomer who was his wife, her life of unfaithfulness and the men that took advantage of her. He could have used the 'exception clause' in his marriage and left her because of her obvious indiscretions, but he took the road less traveled. Hosea continued to stay committed to her because of his love for her. The principle I'm referring to is where God says to Hosea,

> 'I will make her like a desert, turn her into a parched land, and slay her with thirst. I will not show my love to her children, because they are the children of adultery. Their mother has been unfaithful and has conceived them in disgrace.
>
> She said, "I will go after my lovers, who give me my food and my water, my wool and my linen, my olive oil and my drink."
>
> Therefore I will block her path with thornbushes; I will wall her in so that she cannot find her way. She will chase after her lovers but not catch them; she will look for them but not find them.

Then she will say, "I will go back to my husband as at first, for then I was better off than now."[1]

Think of it; what if all the people who left their spouses couldn't find someone else to 'take them in' or be available for them. What if, like Gomer, they too would have to consider going back home or staying out in the world at large as a single person. It gets lonely out there when you're by yourself and you would have a lot of thinking to do about your situation. I have often thought that if two people were left alone, like being on a small deserted island together, they would have to work it out or else not talk to each other for their entire existence on that small spot out in the ocean. I believe that they would have to work it out. Even Tom Hanks eventually had to talk to a volleyball he named 'Wilson'. To avoid the other person and be alone would be harder than just working through it. And that's how marriage should be considered – a small island that is just the domain of the two that inhabit it.

So you're not doing the other person a favor in a marriage gone bad by stepping into it. Stay out of it. As I will say several times in this book, for everyone that leaves a marriage there is generally another that wants them to come back. You don't want to be the one who blocks that possibility. Someone else's marriage is too serious of a thing to mess around with and there will be consequences – in this life or in the life to come. That idea doesn't come from me.

The book of Proverbs gives solemn words for our consideration along these lines.

> 'Men do not despise a thief if he steals to satisfy himself when he is hungry. But if he is found, he will restore sevenfold; he will give all the substance of his house. But whoever commits adultery with a woman lacks understanding; he who does it destroys his own soul.

A wound and dishonor will he get, and his reproach will not be wiped away. *For jealousy is the rage of a man; therefore he will not spare in the day of vengeance. He will not regard any ransom, nor will he rest content, though you give many gifts.*'[2]

If you took a man's wife, even if she was divorced from him, you eliminated any possibility of her coming back home and you destroyed the original family nucleus for the children forever. If as a female you took another woman's husband, it is the same thing. They were not 'free', Jesus says, and they were certainly not yours to take. And ask yourself, do I want to be with someone that would do this to their previous spouse anyway? Is this the kind of person that I want to have my future with?

I am surprised in situations like this that we don't feel more compassion towards a person of our own gender and make-up. Why would a man want to do this to another man? It doesn't make compassionate or moral sense. Why take away another man's future – when you are a man just like him and should know how that would feel? And the same with a woman; why would I, if I were a woman, want to do this to another woman like me – taking her husband and breaking up her family? This is not what a person who is thinking correctly would do. There is no compassionate 'brotherhood' or 'sisterhood' when we act like this. We are not a part of a community of caring people when we act like this, but are only thinking of ourselves, becoming agents of destruction.

It is also interesting to me that we are deluded into thinking that there are two versions of adultery; the regular smutty version and the grace covered version of what some do in our churches. Somehow, as a Christian, when I marry someone that I am not free to take, or I get involved with another when they are not truly free, we think that God's grace will make everything alright because we're operating under forgiveness. We think that a

'Christian' type of second marriage is a different type of infraction and will not come under the world's heading of 'adultery'. How wrong we are. Is there a law of gravity in effect when someone falls out of a tree that is different than a Christian version of gravity that makes it so I don't get hurt when I fall? The hurt, the wounds, the devastation of what were once families, and the collateral damage that comes from all of this still remains the same, Christian or not. The term adultery and the events that follow remain the same – worldly version or church version.

If anything is different, it is that those of the faith should be acting to a higher calling and know that they are subject to a more serious judgement than those who truly didn't know these words that God spoke. We, most of all, should be changing our actions and reflecting the kind of faithfulness that God wants to look down and see. If it is too late to undo for some, not only should they be asking God for forgiveness but asking forgiveness from those they've offended, damaged and destroyed – and make any and all restitutions they can.

Remember, there is another person that usually wanted them to stay. There is also a chorus of other voices crying out too, those of the children cast adrift from the care of their original moms and dads. There are the relatives too. All should be heard out with the hope that you will take a different course of action before you just act in selfishness.

Notes

1. On being alone: Hosea, chapter 2:3-7 [NLT]
2. On another man's wife: Proverbs 5:30-35 [NLT]

In the Shadow of Jesus: the Apostle Paul

I had a former missionary to Taiwan who taught one of my courses in college. Little did I know that this class he was to teach was going to have a major impact on my life.

The course was a New Testament study on the Book of Acts. I remember him looking intently at us from the very beginning. I had seen that look he gave previous to this day. Before I had taken this class I would pass him sometimes in the hall with that same intense projection he gave on his countenance. In passing he usually gave the appearance of a stern and rigid man, and I hoped I'd never have to be in a class of his. How wrong I was about this guy. When he opened up the first class session, he had that the same seriousness about him - but he mixed it with humor, heart, a smile and many of the great life experiences he had from living in a far off place. It didn't take long before I became a strong fan of his.

We were barely a half hour into the lecture when he made, what was for me, a profound statement. It changed my thinking and most importantly my theology.

He said, "Keep in mind that this particular book (Acts) is not a book on doctrine. Things happened from the start that were unique to the situation at hand and were also somewhat personal in their application to those involved at the time. The church was also just beginning, and expanding – so consequently a lot of people were trying to figure things out."

He went on. "Many of the problems that have plagued the church over the years are because people try to make the Book of Acts to be a book on doctrine. They take some of these unique and personal events that belonged to others and consider them to be applicable to their lives also." He paused for a moment to let this important point sink in – then finished his thought. "If you want doctrine – see what Paul ended up saying about all of these events that happened in his various letters to the church as a whole. That's where Paul sorts everything out. He provides order, a proper sense of direction, and from his Biblical knowledge of the Old Testament and the words of Jesus, gives us God's thoughts and insights (doctrine) on these matters."

'Ding' – like a coin dropping into a laundromat slot this statement clicked into my thinking forever. I had been exposed to beliefs like this where people tarried in an upper room because the early disciples did; or felt like Christianity without speaking in tongues certainly meant that you weren't a full-fledged believer. This type of thinking was generally divisive, confusing and usually conflictive with other parts of the Bible. I had been given some keys that morning in our discussion together as a class and I was more appreciative of it than he ever knew.

⌒

Paul was a great man obviously, in many ways, and people have their favorite or most meaningful things about him. When I think of Paul the Apostle I see that he sorted out the things God said and put to rest any uncertainties about their meaning. He gave practical applications to what God spoke about and put shoe leather on them so we could walk them out in our lives. In order to do this he followed a simple guideline of always referencing back to what God said about it first. He didn't speak his mind on any subject to his congregations or followers without first considering what God thought about it.

Old Testament or the words of Jesus – Paul consulted it all before laying out any doctrine or directions to believers. This is an extremely important practice, one that we all should make habit as well. When it comes to spiritual matters, we are not supposed to spin the original message or rationalize it away with our own thoughts or opinions. We are to accurately relate the words and events – the same as anything else we would read or quote. We are called to read the Bible and understand it, not adding too or taking away from it, and figure out how it applies to our lives today. It has done just fine on its own for thousands of years without our 'help'.

I think people feel that the Old Testament prophets of Israel and others added their own stories, tacking on additional messages and more commands to the original 10 that God gave to Moses. This is not true. The Prophets were called to emphasize the original message in various creative and cultural ways; like lying on the ground and making a miniature siege of a town to show in a similar way what was going to happen to Jerusalem in near the future. Another went to the potter's house to see him shape and reshape clay, squashing it occasionally to start afresh if needed, until he got the vessel right. From this example of working with clay he could understand how to speak to Israel on how God wanted to reshape the people and the nation back to a correct moral standard - because they had gotten so far away from the truth.

One of my favorite examples centered on God asking a prophet to marry a prostitute so the man could know what that felt like when she cheated on him. Don't you know that after this, when Hosea spoke to Israel about their unfaithfulness to the God of Jacob, that he spoke with such depth of emotion, compassion and zeal that certainly his message did not escape their attention? They saw the tears and the quavering voice, they knew his personal story, and they certainly heard the words that came from this man whose heart had broken like Gods.

But at the end of the day it was still God's spoken word and His thoughts that got conveyed. This has always been the pattern. God speaks and His faithful messengers convey. They spoke His words in their own way, for sure, but never did they dilute the content, context or original intent.

Paul had respect for these Prophets, but obviously he had a far greater respect for words and person of Jesus, who was the Messiah. God, come down to earth as a man, had spoken and Paul understood his role also to just convey the original message. He, like the prophets before him, followed the pattern. Paul often clarified his position on this matter when he corresponded to the churches by letter, just in case they didn't understand. To the Corinthians, when he wrote to them for a second time, he emphasized again that 'he' wasn't the message but the message bearer.

'You see, we don't go around preaching about ourselves. We preach that Jesus Christ is Lord, and we ourselves are your servants for Jesus' sake.'[1]

So to understand Paul, you must first understand Jesus.

We can say again that Jesus said marriage was only to be terminated because of adultery. We know that this termination clause was not a commandment but a concession to free those who have been completely betrayed and those who can't deal with infidelity any longer. I don't believe it's a commandment because some have worked through unfaithfulness – and families have been saved as a result. Not an easy task but a noble calling if one can do it. There are Biblical examples of this also, the most notable being Hosea, as we have mentioned, in the book that bears his name.

We also know in His silence thereafter that Jesus was saying all other things in marriage can be worked out. He wasn't just speaking for the purpose of giving a command, thinking we needed one more thing to obey just for obedience purposes – no. He knew how important the family was to life and the world. You say, "How do you know this?" If we study scripture will see that the content and context of the Bible bears this truth out. But in case we miss this the larger view, Paul makes it clear in his writings. This is especially true in the discourse he wrote to the Corinthians, coming from the 7th chapter of that first book. We will look at this but I encourage you to read it sometime for yourself.

On this very important subject of marriage and divorce, when Paul wrote the Corinthian church he again emphasized 'not I but the Lord.' The full statement from verse 10 that contains this emphasis goes like this;

> 'But for those who are married, I have a command *that comes not from me, but from the Lord*. A wife must not leave her husband. But if she does leave him, let her remain single or else be reconciled to him. And the husband must not leave his wife'[2]

As he says, he wasn't speaking for himself. If you wonder about the origins of where he got his message from you can read the section again I include on Jesus' comments regarding marriage and divorce, or you can read Jesus' words for yourself in the New Testament. Either way, if you miss this important point about where Paul's teaching came from you will conjecture all sorts of things into Paul's letter that were never intended to be. You even may end up being in opposition, not just to Paul's original intent, but to Jesus' teachings too. That's not a good place to be.

In this famous letter to the Corinthian church, Paul gave some important Christian counsel to those who lived in a Greek culture that was rife with marital and relational confusion. The city of Corinth itself was turned upside down with immorality issues of the deepest kind. Some have called these people the 'messy church' – like we are different somehow and not like them at all. I don't want to diverge to comment on this, but before we can criticize their lives I think we need to be aware of two things.

First, how far had these people come from spiritually to get to where they were when Paul spoke to them? Regardless of one's location in the world or their time in history, in order to appreciate where someone *is* today we have to understand how far they have come *from*. They may not look good to you, but maybe you weren't born in a ghetto or came from the other side of the tracks. Maybe you didn't have to deal with being the first person in your family to complete high school or go to college. Maybe you didn't have to grow up in a culture that had degrading issues or come from a divorced home. Maybe, like my friend Robert, you and I didn't have to compete with half a billion people to get entrance into a college in China that only allowed 3,000 of the best students.

Secondly, we have to consider that most of them only had a portion of the completed message that we have today. They might rise up in unison someday and actually criticize us; asking why we didn't live differently and provide a better Christian example with all the knowledge we had available to us.

The letter Paul wrote was a direct response to some questions the Corinthians had ('Now concerning the things about which you wrote me') so the audience by logic is the church of Christians at Corinth. They wanted to know about the proper bonds of marriage as new believers and I give them credit for this. Theirs was a fairly new church, started in the early years after Christ's coming, and there had been isolated conversions of husbands, wives and children out of larger households. Marriage wasn't going to be a convenient island where all of the natives were the same; no, there were going to be some believing wives now confronted with the aspect of being married to an unbelieving husband, and vice versa.

Once you know this and understand the cultural setting, you will see that the rules for what he is going to say will differ based upon the different responses he expects to get from these two groups. He will write therefore to the Christians and then also address 'to the rest' [non-Christians] in this chapter. He expects the first group will listen to what God says because they love Him – not a far-fetched idea. 'To the rest' he expects they may not listen at all because they are not tied to Christ by love or faith. When you see the context of what Paul wrote about you know that you'd have to have some connection to Jesus to be able to follow these teachings He laid out. Even today they are not easy to follow. I do think, in reality, that these principles Jesus speaks of were meant to apply to everyone, but given their cultural difficulty the first thing many need to do is to recognize and regard the Person who is speaking. This usually comes only by having a heart that is open to God and spiritual things. This also should take place after one receives the gift of salvation, coming from the hand of this same Man who offers it to them. It may be that only in these two cases can we hear, understand, and follow the things Jesus speaks of. You can't clean a fish before you catch it as some say.

So there was a different response Paul expected in Corinth, now that you were following Christ, from what you might have done before. Knowing this, verse 10 would accurately be understood as follows,

'But for those who are married, I have a command that comes not from me, but from the Lord. A **Christian** wife must not leave her husband. But if she does leave

him, let her remain single or else be reconciled to him.
And the **Christian** husband must not leave his wife.'

⌒

There are three messages in this single verse above that are
as follows:

1. Christians should not divorce, even if they cannot stay
    in the situation. I heard lately of a prominent Christian
    couple where one of them abandoned the faith so they
    were going to get a divorce as well. How silly and sad –
    nothing known supports this course of action. A shallow
    faith or confusion on the part of one or both of them
    would be the only normal reason that would allow this to
    happen. That there isn't enough love between them both
    to continue to give a single home to their kids is more
    than disheartening; we need to know that marriage always
    trumps occupational and spiritual differences. In the movie
    Family Man I like where 'Kate' says to Jack that regardless
    of the circumstances, "I choose us." Good words.
    There are many options to avoid divorce but there are
    intolerable situations where some element of protection
    is needed – we need to recognize this. We shouldn't treat
    a temporary separation lightly but we also shouldn't ask
    couples to stay in dangerous circumstances. While people
    may need space to grow up and get their act together, the
    family still has to be given the highest priority.
2. If divorce has taken place, *believers* are not to remarry
    unless death occurs or their spouse has been unfaithful
    with someone else. Sadly, it has often been the opposite –
    'Christians' going off to marry someone else, thinking

that God agrees, and leaving a former spouse to deal with their conduct. I think God's going to deal with this someday and some people are not going to like it.

3. Finally, a Christian is to leave the door open for reconciliation to their original partner if the other hasn't married and being re-united is still a possibility. 'For better or worse, in sickness and in heath, for richer or poorer, 'till death do us part' has its origins in these principles of scripture. We need to consider these words as possibly the most important statement that will be uttered in a marriage ceremony. 'I do' is just a response to this foundational commitment.

Paul emphasizes the same concept of a life time commitment to marriage at the end of this 7th chapter when he says,

'A wife is bound to her husband as long as he lives. If her husband dies, she is free to marry anyone she wishes, but only if he loves the Lord.'[3]

This isn't an isolated reference for he also says in the Book of Romans,

'Now, dear brothers and sisters – you who are familiar with the law – don't you know that the law applies only while a person is living? For example, when a woman marries, the law binds her to her husband as long as he is alive. But if he dies, the laws of marriage no long apply to her. **So while her husband is alive, she would be committing adultery if she married another man.** But if her husband dies, she is free from that law and does not commit adultery when she remarries.'[4]

All this applies equally to men, for we have already seen this portrayed in the words Jesus spoke on men and women dealing with infidelity to their marriages.

The next injunction (1 Corinthians, chapter 7:12 – 14) comes out of a believer being married to an unbeliever – and it doesn't differ from the concept above when it comes to Christian behavior. If the other party is content to live in the marriage you have together, then stay with them. Most likely you either married them in this situation or you came to faith alone under these circumstances. If you did the former then you took that chance out of your belief in love; if you did the latter you came to faith in a situation where you were in the same previous condition that your spouse is now. Either way love should carry the day.

But if the *unbeliever* wants out - then let them go - for it is only an unbeliever in Paul's mind who would ignore the words of Jesus on the importance of marriage. There is a little more depth given here in verses 12 – 14 as to why marriage is important and it has to do with the family. The same concept is given in many other places in the Bible, and one of the more specific passages you can read for yourself is from the Old Testament book of Malachi.[5] Marriage is important to the family because it is important to the future of children and their well-being. It's not just about you or your spouse at some point; you have responsibilities to a few more that are a part of the family unit as well. We talk about the rights of the unborn; well there are the rights of the born as well.

The final injunction (1 Corinthians chapter 7:15 – 17) appeals to the love and compassion that should be within the heart of any Christian person. Paul says that if the unbeliever goes then let them go – the Christian person is not bound to try and work out a marriage that is being abandoned. But what follows is still consistent with regarding marriage as Jesus does. There is still a way to be faithful to love, to your vows, and wanting to save the family for the children's sake. It is such a beautiful appeal and it goes like this;

> 'Don't you wives realize that your husbands might be saved because of you? And don't you husbands realize that your wives might be saved because of you?[6]

The only way that an unbelieving husband or wife could be saved by our conduct is if we displayed some sort of Christian behavior and remained faithful to our vows as long as possible. I don't see how anyone could be influenced to salvation if you abandoned your wayward spouse, abandoned the hope of saving your family, and married someone else. If a spouse is still alive and hasn't committed adultery (sexually engaged with or married to someone else) then the hope of reconciliation is still a possibility. And the question lies hanging in the air under such admittedly impossible circumstances, *how do you know* things won't change? How do you know that in the course of time they won't turn around and change course? *How do you know* that this is the end? You don't. Until they find someone else, if they do, the only option that would leave the door open for redemption is to wait and see what happens. I would think you would want to do this anyway, just on the basis of love.

But can we influence someone else's behavior by our conduct you may say – especially a wayward spouse?

The Apostle Peter, who had himself been greatly influenced by Jesus' faithfulness, patience, and long-suffering with him, said some important things in regards to family relationships on this very issue.

> 'In the same way, you wives must accept the authority of your husbands. Then, even if some refuse to obey the Good News, **your godly lives will speak to**

them without any words. They will be won over by observing your pure and reverent lives.'[7]

'In the same way, you husbands must give honor to your wives. Treat your wife with understanding as you live together. She may be weaker than you are, but she is your equal partner in God's gift of new life. **Treat her as you should so your prayers will not be hindered.**'[8]

'Fathers, do not provoke your children to anger by the way you treat them. Rather, bring them up with the discipline and instruction that comes from the Lord.'[9]

And finally, Jesus says about our relationship with others as we live out our lives in this world,

'You are the light of the world – like a city on a hilltop that cannot be hidden . . . **let your good deeds shine out for all to see, so that everyone will praise your heavenly Father.**'[10]

You will be an example – either for good or bad – and there is no neutral ground, as much as you may seek to find it. What you choose to be is solely up to you.

~

So, let's think for a moment. Should the response of our churches today, to this teaching, be any different than those to whom Paul wrote to in Corinth? How could we say that we have other options that they didn't?

I want to take a look at this in the chapter that follows.

Notes

1. Paul was not the message: The New Testament – 2 Corinthians, chapter 4:5 (NLT)
2. On marriage: The New Testament – 1 Corinthians, chapter 7:10 (NLT)
3. The obligation to the living spouse: The New Testament – 1 Corinthians, chapter 7:39 (NLT)
4. Free while a husband is living?: The New Testament – Romans, chapter 7:1–3 [NLT]
5. The importance of the family: The Old Testament – Malachi, chapter 2:15
6. The importance of influencing a possible reconciliation: The New Testament – 1 Corinthians 7:16 [NLT]
7. A wife's influence on a husband: The New Testament – 1 Peter 3:1-2 [NLT]
8. A husband's influence on his wife: The New Testament – 1 Peter 3:7 [NLT]
9. A father's influence on his children: The New Testament – Ephesians 6:4 [NLT]
10. Our influence on the world: Jesus – The New Testament – Matthew 514-16 [NLT]

So What's Happening Today?

I think there are a few reasons why people give up on their marriages in general and also the marriages of those in the churches of today. This is not comprehensive, but if you can get these things right I think you'll be in pretty good shape.

1. **Ignorance**: I believe that many just don't know what the devastation will be until they errantly step into this place of divorce and hurt. I have seen many condone this course of action and say it's no big deal. But regardless of the bravado that surrounds their strong opinions, statements like this contain shallow or not existent evidence. But if you are willing to step out on your own and know more of the truth ahead of time, may I recommend three great books to you.
    a. *The Unexpected Legacy of Divorce* by Judith Wallerstein, Julia Lewis and Sandra Blakeslee.
    b. *The Case Against Divorce* by Diane Medved, Ph.D.
    c. *The Bible*: I don't reference this great book just to be religious – I recommend it because it is steadfast in its commitment to marriage. I ask anyone to show me where it ever condones divorce, especially in the way we go about it today.

2. **What isn't being taught and what is being accepted**: We may not be hearing the full story from people's lives and from the pulpit there might be too much silence in

churches today. Many in society rationalize their behavior and these things are not being taught very much in Christianity anymore either. I think the whole subject is too flammable, given the decisions made by many we know in and outside the church. Most leaders and pastors stay away from these difficult truths. However, we still have the responsibility to be true to the facts if we are educated people from all walks of life. In Christianity we also have a responsibility to be true to scripture and what it says. We can't blame our churches for lack of communication and people around us that give us bad advice; we need to choose to be on solid ground because it's important to *us*. This means we'll have to do our own research if we're secular, or if we're Christians, we'll need to know the true context of the Bible for ourselves.

3. **A lack of creativity, imagination and perseverance**: When faced with overwhelming circumstances, boredom or discouragement in his life, my brother Bryan would encourage himself to have a little bit more imagination about his situation. There are a lot of options rather than divorce but it seems people lack creativity on how to deal with their circumstances. If this is hard to do in moments of discouragement, surround yourself with those who can look at your life and help you in positive ways. Get a book, get alone to pray, review positive solutions on the internet – but don't give up. It is the easy way out – but you can show care, imagination and perseverance by being strong enough to take a different approach. Paul the Apostle told Timothy,

> 'Timothy, guard what what has been entrusted to you. Avoid godless, foolish discussions with those who oppose you with their so-called knowledge.'[1]

4. **A misunderstanding of the concept of Grace**: This is
    probably one of the most deceptive concepts of them
    all, as it takes a word meant for a specific purpose and
    tries to shoe horn it into any and all applications. Like
    Cinderella's sisters, there are those who attempt to
    make the glass slipper fit their situation when it clearly
    doesn't.

    Grace is almost always used in conjunction with our
    having an unmerited entrance to heaven through Christ,
    which is the opposite of a salvation that is based upon our
    own character or works of goodness. We could never enter
    those gates without an infinite amount of grace that can
    only come from our Savior. This is the basis of heaven's
    economy entirely.

    But I don't really find anywhere where grace is used
    as a blanket that is supposed to cover the wrong behavior
    that we knowingly do. One of my favorite musicians, who
    will always remain so, left his family to marry someone
    who left their family in the same way. When confronted
    by this on occasion he'll tell those in attendance that they
    don't understand 'grace.' I think it is the other way around
    actually. Grace, when used as a reference to our behavior,
    is always the ability to be a better person than I could ever
    be without God's help.

    'Timothy, my dear son, be strong through the grace
    that God gives you in Christ Jesus', Paul says to his
    younger protégée.[2]

    There is a strength we have available to us to act
    differently than we normally would - if we are *Christians*.
    There are those who are only religious at best and try to
    deny by their actions that there is a power available in the
    Christian faith to do right.[2] There are also those who are
    just being deceptive about their behavior.[3]

How could Jesus say, 'It is better that I leave because the Helper is going to come . . .' if no help showed up after that? So if you're going to use the word grace, which has Biblical origins for sure, please use it as it's intended to be used and not as an excuse for poor life choices. This is a total misapplication of its meaning.

5. **You're an unbeliever who's living without God's direction**: Paul said that only the unbelievers are allowed to walk away – out of stubbornness, unwillingness to follow what is good, an ignorance of God's ways or hardness of heart. I would have to assume this if I saw no effort otherwise.

    A subject Jesus mentioned often was to just be aware that we'll be among unbelievers when we're at church. I think we ought to have unbelievers at church that will question everything rationally and openly. I'm not asking you to look for them but be aware of this. On the other hand the Kingdom of God will also appear larger than it is and there will be tares among the wheat. So if you walk away from your marriage and call yourself a believer in Jesus, what am I supposed to think about your faith and your beliefs? As importantly, what is your husband, your children, and your community supposed to think of your faith? Would it be valid for them to think your belief system is either a convenience or a joke? I think that is a possibility. I'm not saying this to hurt you if you are thinking this; I'm just saying some self-examination to know your true spiritual condition would be appropriate in this circumstance.

6. **Love**: I think that some spouses have never really truly loved the person that they were with or learned how to.

Getting married often becomes the focus in dating and then people rush ahead instead of taking the time to know the other person. The most important thing is learning about love and knowing whether or not you have it for this person. This is going to take some time.

Once we learn about love and what it means to commit my life to this person, then marriage is the proper next step. Marriage is as easy as falling off of a log, as some say, but love and loving deeply has to come first. Maybe that's the problem – we didn't show or know how to love. I don't think that's an acceptable excuse for exiting a marriage because we can learn how to love if we are willing. Paul speaks in this same Corinthian letter (chapter 13) about love being patient, kind and never failing. Wouldn't this be an ideal time to show your love or learn how to love? I think so. Or what do you have to offer the next person - your affection and commitment as long as everything goes perfectly?

7. **Faith in the face of the impossible**: There were over 5,000 people on a hillside and Jesus had been teaching for most of the day. As the day wore on it became increasingly more uncomfortable to the disciples however to subconsciously know that these people had to go home to eat – yet Jesus continued to speak. It was easy to see that people were drinking it in and needed to hear what he said; still children were beginning to cry from impending hunger and at best everyone was going to miss dinner even if He stopped now. The disciples approached Him gingerly about this but at the same time didn't hide their concern.

When the disciples asked about who was going to feed all these people who had come to hear Him, I like Jesus' response. He said to the disciples, "You feed them."[4] What a staggering statement.

So before we finish this story, I want to say that we generally see our limitations as being God's too so we quit when it gets too difficult for us. I had done things this way for many years but I began to wonder why. Why need God for anything if He can only do what I can do? I'm not saying that everything will go your way if you pray but at least ask and give Him time to respond. For since that time I have seen some incredible stuff turned around when I allowed myself to believe in God's power when my faith and my efforts had run aground.

Back to the hillside we left. Jesus clearly wanted them involved, though it was totally beyond their ability. Secondly He asked them to bring what little they had to Him, then sit down and watch. We can see in what followed that God doesn't call us to impossible things on our own but He can work out things that we cannot, if we will just watch and wait. His challenge for them to feed the multitude was a really a lifetime lesson for them to bring things to His feet that they wouldn't be able to solve and then trust Him with the results.

Bad relationships and impossible break-ups seem to be unsolvable and 'irreconcilable' too – but the same truth that came from a hillside applies to us as well. We need to allow for the impossible. We need to trust Him with our unsolvable concerns and wait for Him to work. His joy is to finally hear from you in prayer on something like this, maybe for the first time, and not have you walk away.[5] An improvement in our prayer lives might be part of what we needed all along. It's really the only way that you solve some of the most disturbing pieces of your life. Turn to Him.

〜

I don't see God being OK with divorce in society or in the church today. I want to speak to the church for a moment by asking a few questions.

If we have errored as believers, why don't we admit it? Why are we offended by the suggestion that we have blown a serious hole in our Christian faith by what we've done? And why do we undermine the faith and marriages of those around us by pretending our decisions were OK with God and these values we're talking about don't count anymore? If we have married again in disobedience, why can't we go back to former spouses and our children, if possible, and at least ask for forgiveness for our bad decisions. I have sadly heard some say that God didn't want them to live in an 'unbelieving marriage' so He allowed them to leave and had blessed them with a 'Christian spouse' instead. This is as much garbage as it is damaging and an infinitely poor witness as well. Do we wonder why some don't darken the doors of our churches? Heavens.

The proper role of the believing spouse shown here, be it a man or a woman, is to act as a sanctifying influence in the marriage and in the home, especially for the sake of the children. It doesn't mean you have to live in a drunken, physically abusive, demeaning or dangerous situation – but it does mean that you don't forsake your marriage unless it forsakes you.

$\backsim$

There are many families that have encouraged me over the years when they responded to their own dark times with a faithful commitment to Christ. I have seen couples come back together from impossible situations in their marriages, and even in their divorces, to be reunited again. I have also seen many that have regretted their hasty decisions not to wait, finding that the other side of the hill had just as many weeds as the one they came from, with less common benefits than the first marriage had.

As I have said before, the first marriage is the one I believe that God will bless the most – believer or not. It is where the lives of the children are forever bound up. It is the family that is rooted in the original parents, grandparents, and extended relatives. This nucleus, whenever possible, is the best place for all of us to be.

Notes

1. Guard what is entrusted to you / Paul to Timothy: The New Testament – 1 Timothy, chapter 6:20 [NLT]
2. Be strong Timothy because of God's grace / Paul: The New Testament – 2 Timothy, chapter 2:1 [NLT]
3. Acting religious but denying the power God gives to change: The New Testament – 2 Timothy, chapter 3:5 [NLT]
4. The misapplication of grace by some: The New Testament – Jude, chapter 1:3-4 [NLT]
5. "You feed them": The New Testament – Matthew, chapter 14:13-16 [NLT]
6. The rich young ruler walks away from the impossible: The New Testament – Luke, chapter 18:18-27 [NLT]

Is He For Or Against?

When we talk about all this, realize that Jesus isn't personally against anyone, wanting to pick a fight with us for no reason. He isn't against us at all. I don't think we see or understand His intentions correctly at times. It usually isn't what He is against that should cause us discomfort, but what He is for that should be the focus of our concern.

He cares about hurt hearts that have been left behind by the other partner, through the broken vows of marriage. He cares about the original family and how its abandonment, for whatever cause, has affected the lives of all those involved - forever. He cares about those who were too young to defend themselves against the actions of their parents and had to suffer the most. He cares about these same 'children' who are older now, old enough to supposedly understand, but who still don't fathom the issues that surrounded the divorce and will always miss the parents they should have had. He is for the truth, which means He is against lying – especially when the lies are coming from the mouths of those who are not being honest about their disobedience.

Someone very close to me used to say that he liked 'having all the cards on the table.' I agree. I know God prefers that we be honest by having the real story on the table for others to see. If we can't do this, then I think there is something wrong. There is something we are ashamed of – something, even after many years that we are still trying to hide. It is time to come out of hiding and not cloak the actions of the past behind the curtain of deception any more.

If you can change the mistakes of the past, please do so. If you are considering a new relationship with someone who shouldn't be out and 'available', don't be in the line of fire between Him and what He cares about. Get out of the way and ask for His help to stay out of the way. If you are past this point, deal with it properly and get the forgiveness of those you've hurt. You rebelled openly, now deal with it in the same way, openly and honestly. I hope within the confines of your home that you and your current spouse will seriously ask God for His forgiveness and change the outcome as best as you can. You can't brush Him or His principles away just because you feel safe and accepted in your church – that won't work either. Though the damage has been done good changes can take place, but it will only come through your obedience this time.

CHAPTER **8**

Separation - Apart for a Purpose

Separation - Apart for a Purpose

"Separation will tell you all you need to know about the other person."

Michael Pleasant

Separation - Apart for a Purpose

"If you're going through hell, keep going."

Winston Churchill

Separation - Apart for a Purpose

It is interesting to me as to how much God values relationships; yours with Him, His with you and the way you interact with others. It may surprise you that He values proper relationships more than He does church. He's not against church obviously, as He died to create our ability to approach Him ourselves and wants us to gather together with other believers. But just as the people are more important than the walls and plaster of our hallowed halls, so is our relationship with Him and others more important than how we stand up and sit down, sing our songs of worship, or bow our heads in solemn prayer.

Consider the following statement from the Book of Malachi;

'Another thing you do: You flood the Lord's altar with tears. You weep and wail because He no longer looks with favor on your offerings or accepts them with pleasure from your hands. You ask, "Why?"

It is because the Lord is the witness between you and the wife of your youth. You have been unfaithful to her, though she is your partner, the wife of your marriage covenant.'[1]

Consider also what Jesus is recorded as saying in the Book of Matthew;

"Therefore, if you are offering your gift at the altar and there remember that your brother or sister has something against you, *leave your gift there in front of the altar. First go and be reconciled to them; then come and offer your gift.*"[2]

The first verse says your worship and the prayers you make at church are useless if you have forsaken your marriage commitment to your wife [and husband]. All the religion in the world is useless if matters aren't right at home. Peter reflects these same sentiments in the New Testament as well, saying,

> 'In the same way, you husbands must give honor to your wives . . . Treat her as you should so your prayers will not be hindered.'[3]

The same again would also apply to wives in respect to their husbands.

The other verse in Matthew logically follows the message of the first, telling us to leave our gifts and offerings at church, get up and walk out the door if we need to, and get things right with those whom we should love – even if it's a neighbor. The blessing we will get when we return to church will be far greater than if we had stayed. People would look at Christianity differently today if we practiced this priority of regarding our relationships with others as being a part of our worship. If we made our services contingent on 'getting things right' with people, what differences would we see with mankind and in our world? This is exactly what He is saying.

Is it any wonder then that God is grieved when we have divorce in our midst? Do you think it bothers Him when we just go on with our worship and pretend that the damage done to our families is a separate issue, not related to our walk with Him? I don't even have to guess personally, I'm sure of it. I am concerned because of this. I think we're ignoring something big and important from God's point of view called marriage and the family.

〜

I anticipate that I will be misunderstood when I advocate separation for couples that are having severe issues in their marriage. But I believe there are tough situations where it is best for couples to be apart for a while. I personally would much rather advocate separation, with a commitment to work it out, than the destructive thinking that is being put out today about divorce by many who should know better – pastors, clergy, marriage and family counselors, and people of all walks of life - religious or not. In a lot of cases, what we see happening to marriages in our midst is just ignored by all in attendance. Some leaders find it way too volatile to address this topic, especially if they want to keep their congregations or their jobs.

So instead of Jesus allowing adultery as the only reason for divorce, many of us have extended His list. We must certainly think we know better than He. Are we adding His supposed endorsement to our choices when we ignore His words and true intentions? I don't see anywhere where He spoke of these options we are now so readily advocating.

What we can see today in the world, in Christianity too, is the following:

"Did he hit you? Get a divorce."

"Is he out of work like before? Get a divorce."

"Was she shouting and screaming at the kids again? Get a divorce."

"Has he or she dropped their Christian faith? Get a divorce."

"Has your partner gained some weight or having emotional difficulties? Get a divorce."

"Does either of you have a drinking, smoking or substance abuse problem? Get a divorce."

"Are the children in danger? Get a divorce."

"Are you both seemingly going different ways? Get a divorce."

"Are you just not getting along anymore? Get a divorce."

"You deserve better than what you have! Get a divorce!"

Admittedly, none of the situations above are good and one or two require immediate removal from the relationship in my opinion - but I don't believe the answer to any of these is divorce. Just because people have problems doesn't mean that commitment couples have should be terminated. How destructive have we been with the recommendations we've made from the pulpit, in professional counseling, and in our casual personal talks with others, when we have based everything on our opinions. We have thrown out, like popcorn, what we think is wise advice on the real life situations people are facing all around us. I personally don't want to be a part of this dangerous circle of public opinion.

Because of this, however, many will stand at the crossroads seeing only one path, feeling like divorce is the only option and the only way out for them. Most all in society around us seemingly agree with this singular path of no return when things get difficult. It appears that all grievances, like tags on Christmas packages, seemed to be marked with the label 'Divorce Only' on them. That there is only a singular option like this is not true; that is why I am writing this book. The concept of separation, and the difference it can make when it's coupled with commitment, is hardly known or uttered anymore. It is truly the forgotten option.

So which way do we go?

Know that somewhere, ages and ages hence, this choice we make and the road we take may have the biggest impact on our lives of all the things we'll do. And not just impact us, but also the people around us and the generations ahead of us that will be affected, though we may never know them or ever see them.

⤿

So if your marriage is in trouble and you are not together now, you are probably already separated. That part is done. You're away from them and they from you, so why not just stop for a moment where you're at? You are already free from the situation; you don't need to look for more freedom if you're already *free*. There may be some financial stuff to work out, separate accounts and new bills to deal with, and you may lose a few shared material and monetary assets for the time being, but you accomplished your goal. You removed yourself from the situation that was unhealthy for you and maybe for your kids also. You have already taken the road called *Separation*, now bed down for the night and wait for a clearer view tomorrow.

It will be important going forward to seek out fellowship and friendship with those who can help you. You want friends who are supportive of your marriage, and therefore those you can trust, so you can clear your mind properly. Nothing is lost while you make a careful, clear, non-impulsive and non-reactive decision. Spend some time with yourself, committed friends and God also so you can sort things out. Just don't pursue divorce is my recommendation, and please do not date. If the one who hurt you calls, put them on hold for a while and tell them you'll get back to them when you're ready. Slow your heart rate down and take steady breaths.

There is no need at this point to run down into the valley of loss that few come back from.

⤿

As I share all of this, I want to be clear on several things.

Separation is never a good thing to advocate up front to anyone, as there are some stresses, hardships, temptations and dangers involved that you may not be prepared for at this time. However, like those who came out west on the Oregon Trail in the 1800's, you may have to make the journey – prepared or not. I'm just saying that separation should not be considered the first line of defense, but the next logical step, after many others that came before it, for a marriage that is in deep trouble. Remember that if this whole thing looks bad, temporarily being apart for a purpose is a hopeful, reconciliatory decision that can turn things around.

We hear of dire situations in marriages where our immediate reaction is to say that divorce must be the answer. But if you are of the faith and study the Bible at all, you should struggle with this idea – or you should study the topic again. The more you get around families, up and close, that have chosen divorce – the more this kind of self-wisdom, often offered, turns sour when acted upon. Hopefully common sense and conviction will arise to say that there has to be a better way.

There is a better way. For crisis situations, in times of extreme difficulty, it is separation instead of divorce that is a better answer, with the focus of staying faithful to your loved ones and your vows while you both work it out.

Before we get into some practical aspects of this application, let me tell you about an important experience I had that relates to this concept.

Notes

1. On church and relationships: The Old Testament – Malachi, chapter 2:13 – 14 [NIV]
2. On church and relationships: The New Testament – Matthew, chapter 5:23 – 24 [NIV]
3. On prayer and relationships: The New Testament – 1 Peter, chapter 3:7 [NLT]

A Village in Nairobi

I didn't know that this was going to be a life changing moment, but it was. Do you know when these moments are going to come along? Maybe you do, but I don't; they have all been unique and wonderful surprises to me. I only see them clearer through the rear view mirror after time has come and gone, viewing these moments against the backdrop of the other life experiences I've had.

⌒

I waited in her office wondering if this was going be a good thing. As my own doctor was farther away in Idaho, and because of his recommendation to do so, I was trying to find a doctor who was more local to where I was currently employed. The person I was going to see today was a woman.

I don't usually feel comfortable as a man to have a woman doctor, but she had been highly recommended by a fellow on our aerospace production line. I was interested in meeting her. I was waiting outside her office in a small reception area. Hers was a set-up where two professionals shared the waiting room, each having their own adjacent office nearby. You could see that there was a budgeted effort going on here. Before long she came out and invited me in.

She was darker in skin color than I, and her name and accent spelled out that she wasn't from Seattle or the United States but from a different country. I was to find out on this visit that she came from Africa originally – Nairobi I believe. It was amazing to be with her, not so much for the doctor stuff, though she was as good as anyone else, but it was the small talk we had about her county of origin between examination questions that was interesting to me.

It was at some point during the visit that we talked about the problems in marriages today, which is a passionate subject for me. I told her of some of my experiences and observations as an American, then she spoke to me of her culture and the small village in Africa that she was raised in. Ultimately she finished by speaking about her mom and dad.

In our American culture there are definite cases of intolerable abuses in marriage, with spouses and with children. However, most of the abuses I've seen and heard about in my smaller circle of friends and associates just seem to be wimpy and selfish excuses to leave a marriage. Maybe there are still a lot of life situations that I haven't been exposed to yet. That afternoon however, when she spoke of her father's physical abuse of her mother, it was the real thing. It wasn't the American version she spoke of, but the African version, and I remember her statements weren't fake or over exaggerated.

She said, "In my culture divorce is not acceptable and it is looked down upon. We lived in a smaller village and everyone was very inter-connected. For a husband and wife to divorce in our village was very rare, as it impacted all of the families involved and affected those in the community too. So when my dad got physically abusive, my mom decided to take vacations – long ones. She would leave the furniture in their home, keep her last name and keep the same address, but mom would pack up her clothes and come see me or my sister. She wasn't going to come back until he changed. On one trip out of the country, she spent a year and a half with me during my graduate program at college. My mom would tell him each and every time she left that she wasn't going to put up with his abuse." I didn't hear in her story that her father was an unfaithful man, just that he was just abusive.

I admired her mom's stick-to-it-iveness and of her story of courage. To stay married to this guy and uphold the beliefs of her community, however backwards it may seem to us, was noble in my opinion. I also liked hearing about the importance of marriage in her culture, the priority of parents and families staying together. I wasn't sure of where this was going next, except maybe a permanent vacation status for her mother.

"Do you know how it turned out?" she eventually said, looking at me with her usual kind smile.

I couldn't even guess. I shook my head no.

"Well . . . . . today you can't get them apart."

I still get emotional thinking about the end of this story of impossibility and desperation, where maybe the heavens above parted and God interceded for what you would call an amazing woman. It was worth the price of admission to hear of this family, and the faith, love and courage of her mother. You could see that though far away from her village and its influences, she was deeply affected by the final outcome of her parent's marriage and her mother's example.

How does this differ from our culture? I think we feel as Americans that we have life all figured out, but I don't see enough evidence to believe this is true regarding marriage in our culture. Instead of thinking of the forgotten option of long vacations while one maintains their commitment, we only have two options to pick from it seems. Our decisions seem to be only black or white, married or divorced, you're in or you're out. But there is another option represented here in my doctor's story and I think it is a wiser direction worth considering.

To many it would be crystal clear that her mom should have left her dad for good. However, there possibly is a different way to look at it, and maybe God looks at it differently too. Again, after only listing adultery as the justifiable reason for divorce, I see Jesus saying that all other issues can be worked out in some other way. It is the answer that He gave out of silence.

The psalmist, speaking about God's viewpoint when looking at our actions, wrote,

> "When you did these things and I kept silent, **you thought I was exactly like you**. But I now will arraign you and set My accusations before you."[1]

My conclusion is I think God thinks differently than a lot of people do on these issues. I don't think it's a question of being African or American either, but more of a question of what is right and what is wrong? And though some separation needed to take place in her mom's situation, indefinitely if that's what it might have taken, I think her mom was right in the way she responded to their situation. She not only redeemed a marriage, a wayward man, and a watching community – but she redeemed her family too. This is not Pollyanna version of some fairy tale I came up with, but a real life story I relate to you.

As odd as it may sound to our American ears, we may need a revival back to marriage as it was intended to be, back to love as it was meant to endure and faithfulness as it was meant be shown.

I want to end this book talking about the things we may need to make this journey toward faithfulness and what it may take to turn our lives around.

Notes

1. When God's silent, does it mean He approves?: The Old Testament – Psalm 50:21 [NIV]

CHAPTER **9**

Our Needs

Our Need To Communicate

"Never miss an opportunity to shut up."

Mark Twain

Our Need To Communicate

"The single biggest problem in communication is the illusion that it has taken place."

George Bernard Shaw

Our Need to Communicate

Look communication up in the dictionary and you'll see that it involves many ways to reach another human being with a message.

There have been so many good communicators before us and behind us that we really have no excuse. I think of Confucius and other ancient wisdom givers; there are also the Greek philosophers, Roman poets and orators of days gone by. These examples from history are not meant to exclude the many contemporary authors and speakers of our time.

I also think of Jesus; of all His words and His use of parables. For parables, He used the everyday things of life around us. Through these natural illustrations He spoke to us in ways we *could* understand so that we could catch a glimpse of things we didn't understand – like heaven and values that are important to God in this life. If you could gauge a speaker's greatness by the number of lives they affected, again, He stands alone.

He also heard and saw people with a purposeful intent. He understood a lot about them without having to ask, by using careful observation. He of course had an advantage, being God as a man, but He still cared enough to notice the most detailed things about us. Like an expert surgeon, He wanted to know where to carefully insert Himself and why.

Isaiah said about Him,

'Out of the stump of David's family will grow a shoot –
yes, a new Branch bearing fruit from the old root. And

the Spirit of the Lord will rest on Him . . . *He will not judge by appearance, nor make a decision based on hearsay. He will give justice to the poor and make fair decisions for the exploited.*'[1]

This speaks to the most intimate communications possible; that of our being known from the inside out by Him. We can trust He will not crush us or inflict hurt unnecessarily. Like the expert surgeon He is, He is careful in all He does.

⟿

When you reach out to someone, you are going to use some kind of a *vehicle* to transfer the information with. Speaking with our voices is the primary avenue of communication as it allows us to take various letters of the alphabet and create enough words and meanings to fill endless libraries.[2] But words were made to be enhanced. Like a caboose behind a train, you can couple your words with a tone of voice, a pause, a question, a hand or a foot gesture. You can add music, touch, visuals, graphics, photographs, quotes and other references from everyday life around us. As part of this, communication is listening as well. We can improve our listening skills along with our speaking skills to understand better. All of these combined can make the difference between success or failure in getting our message properly conveyed to others. But when we use only our voice, we can fail to properly express what we're trying to get across.

Given this, there is another form of communication not mentioned that we may have used many times with our children when we were disciplining them. It is our absence from them and their absence from us. When we send them into the corner or have them go to their room, they can't see or be with us.

Children don't usually enjoy being alone, especially when they're away from mom and dad. When they are out of the family circle, even for a moment, they are missing the fun the others are having. This form of communication, called 'time out', is for the purpose of having them be left alone long enough for them to think about their behavior. If sufficient impact is made in this way, we catch the attention of our children for good. If situations arise, subsequent issues either become non-existent or easier to deal with next time.

I think the same thing can be done with adults. We're not too old to be reached or corrected in this way.

When there are heated arguments in a marriage it is good to take a short break and walk away for a time. This is a 'mini' separation of sorts, which may help you both to calmly come back to the table to alleviate larger problems. It helps all of us to stop and cool off before any additional damage is done. You still have to deal with the issues and they don't go away, as much as you'd like them to, but hopefully you've thought it out properly and you're in a better frame of mind to make concessions or think of new solutions together. However, if things go seriously wrong in a marriage, isolation from the family for a longer time might be needed. You may need to communicate to your spouse through isolation that things need to change drastically.

Keep in mind that our children never think in terms of total banishment from us forever when they go off to be alone. They usually don't have the thought of never seeing us again – that doesn't even enter into the equation for them. I see the same principle in marriage. If we can love our children in this way, never letting them think that we'd ever leave them, why can't we share the same commitment and depth of love toward our spouse? Doesn't the relationship of being a couple come before having children together? Give it the same priority then.

Using isolation or separation, our spouse may need to know in the strongest way possible:

a. That their drinking habits are unacceptable and you are going to stay away until they get help to get sober for good.

b. That they need to hold a job. You are letting them know that you are going to take your end of the finances and give them their remaining resources, if they exist, but they are going to have to learn that it takes money and a job to survive in this world. They may have to starve, or exhaust their friendships until they figure this out, but they cannot return until they do.

c. That their constant condescending comments or threatening physical behaviors are unacceptable in the house you share together. They are not welcome back into your life until they can learn how to speak kindly and respectfully, and they are certainly not welcome back until they can control their temper. They can return when you feel safe around them.

d. That the pictures they look at, or sites that they frequent, are not acceptable anymore and never were. Until they are committed solely to you and not looking upon the body of another person, man or woman, they are not welcome in your life anymore.

There may be more that would pertain to your situation, but you get the idea.

If you were to take this kind of a stance against unacceptable behavior, but also take an equal stance for your marriage when doing this, I believe that you would have the support of every good friend and family member that you know. Not only would it be a good example to others, winning many to your cause, but you may get your family back together as well. That is the single and ultimate goal of this whole thing anyway – restoring the family unit. You may even start a revival within the marriages of your town or neighborhood; marriages that are asking for changed behavior and a new level of commitment, but are nonetheless steadfast in their desire to stay together.

The added benefit is that you will be a better communicator at the end of this exercise and a stronger person. You also will have helped your spouse to clearly understand the issues between you that constant complaining would have never accomplished. You will know in the future that you have the ability *together* to nip serious behaviors in the bud, and if there is a next time [hopefully not], you will be listened to more seriously on these issues. If you aren't, you just follow the same steps again until you are. This becomes a marriage skill, one that will keep you safe and keep the situation from ever going too far again. It is a skill that you will also be able to extend to others who need the same support in their marriages.

When you don't take steps like these but just let things go, I think you're asking for failure. If you get frustrated, because you're only talking, and then exit the marriage, I believe you were a poor communicator and faithless. I believe that you showed the world that you were not committed. Your spouse's serious situation may give license by some to your position of leaving, but the destruction of your family will linger for life. This will happen to your kid's for sure and possibly for future generations to come.

Admittedly the dire situation you find yourself in may not be your fault, but the solution could be in your hands. If you think that your spouse has become totally incompetent or has serious issues, is this the time to leave them forever? The outcome is ultimately going to be their decision, but I hope that those who love them would extend every opportunity possible for them to be restored to the family unit and brought to wholeness as well. I believe it is what the sane would do for the insane.

Remember that separation, if done correctly, is a training ground for returning to our marriages. Everything mentioned, even the times apart, are to be taken from a large scale of problems back into a smaller set of disciplines and principles to be used within the marriage. Any problem can be a solution if looked at correctly, and accomplish the ultimate goal of having you all back home and together again.

Notes

1. Jesus not judging from outside appearances, but from within: The Old Testament – Isaiah, chapter 11:1-4 [NLT]
2. There is no end to the books that could be written: Ecclesiastes 12:9-12

Our Need to be Patient and Reflective

I was invited to go to a writer's circle once, though I didn't really know what that was. A writer's circle was a small gathering of potential writers who bring a portion of what they are working on, maybe a small chapter or section of their literary composition, and the other writers are allowed to critique their work. I was invited to participate even though I was new and didn't have a section of this book to bring at the time.

Initially I subconsciously assumed two things. One, I assumed that this was going to be light hearted and very constructive – and secondly, I assumed that I was among a group of very good writers or at least humble aspiring writers. Names were exchanged and hello's made, but before I had even sat down and got comfortable, the older lady across the table from me asked,

"So, you're a writer?"

"I have a book called The Forgotten Option that I'm working on", I said, "so yes, I guess I am."

"How do you know it's any good?" she asked.

Wow, my first meeting and I was face to face with Earnest Hemingway in disguise.

I gathered myself a bit and told her, "My Publisher thought it is going to be a very important subject and they are looking forward to my finishing it."

"You have a publisher?" she said, a bit taken back.

"I do," I replied. That seemed to stop this intimidating investigation and her apparent effort to establish herself as the resident expert of this gathering.

That's how the night started and we had only begun.

⌐

It was exciting to me to be able to read everyone's material and give any insights I could in a positive way. I decided on the spot to use a 3 phased approach; to give each person an opening greeting, tell them next what was good about their offered selection and finally, in as low key a way as possible, offer a short list of suggestions from my vantage point that could be evaluated by each writer later on.

I can't remember all of the information in each story, but I do remember that the hardest part of the whole evening was the last reading.

There was this small, very sweet young gal that was going to college and writing her own science fiction novel on the side. I remember that her character development in the writing she brought was so well done. It was about an adventurous daughter of an 'alien' family that liked to push the borders of her little valley that she called home a bit further each day. 'Careon' [I'll give her character that name because I can't remember what the original was] was a mildly defiant, adventurous and courageous young lady who had a spirit of joy about her – maybe like her author. Everything about Careon pushed her forward into her life; to the edges of her valley she called home and out in the world beyond.

It seemed to me that I could sense this young author and her story were going to be good.

As her character went about the purposeful exploration of her valley in this first chapter, and peeked at the horizons beyond, the writing of this young woman next to me was so good you could smell the fauna and feel the dirt trail that her character was walking on. I could sense the heartbeat of adventure within the character of Careon that she was developing. I seemingly saw the bright skies above her, and touched each leaf and palm branch in the forest that brushed against her body as she explored the tropical valley she called home. It was magnificent – I was already thinking for the first time that night that I would buy this kind of a book and was thankful to be meeting its author early on. Her writing was just so pure. It was without any romantic overtones that some feel they need to keep a reader interested these days. The whole thing was refreshing.

As we went around the room while each critiqued her work, I was confused and felt alone in my assessment of the young lady's work. I was surprised when each critiqued her that I heard nothing flattering from the group in general on her composition. I was then completely stunned when the second to the last writer ripped her to pieces.

She said to this young lady, advertising herself as a science fiction expert because she had read a lot of them (?) that this kind of science fiction style that she had presented to the group was out of date. She said the whole thing was going to have to change. I was floored. As it all unfolded, I had to endure an egotistical and brutal evaluation of this young lady's work. It was beyond odd to me that this current evaluator who was going full guns had written the worst piece of the evening. She finally ended her blunt and unloving critique by offering her email to the young lady, evidently so she could 'modestly' help my young friend to write a better piece. The blind was going to guide the one with crystal clear vision and a skillful pen out of the supposed ditch she was in. It was too much to take in.

But the oddest thing I remember is at the end of this critique is this young lady bowed her head in complete submission to the evaluation she had just been given, clapping her hands lightly together in some kind humble gesture, oddly thankful for the beating she just received from the Pulitzer Prize winner at the end of the table.

Interestingly enough, I was the last person in line to critique this young lady's work. I took a deep breath before starting to share with her my thoughts.

I told this young lady that her character development was excellent and I that could feel the spirit of Careon 'the adventurer' coming from her pages. I let her know that in my opinion her description of the valley and the tropical forest was so good that I could not only see it in my mind's eye but feel the plants against my own skin as I walked along with Careon, so to speak.

It may have been a bit harsh for those assembled, but the second to the last thing I told her was that her work was head and shoulders above anything else that had been presented that evening. I didn't look up or shift my gaze toward the others, as I think it would have been a little suicidal.

She didn't humbly clap after I spoke. I remember she was so dumbfounded by my contrary opinion that she could barely focus on what I was saying. Maybe no one ever told her how good she was, and maybe she was just used to getting whippings by now. She just looked dazed and it appeared in this moment that some of the color had left her face.

The last thing I said to her *emphatically* was, "Don't change a thing."

I hope that she kept her style. What she had written was amazing. I thought she may have been a bit gifted for sure, but definitely unique in her style of storytelling as well. I would like to believe that a ray of light penetrated her soul; that maybe she would find a bit of courage to be herself for what was sure to be the long journey ahead.

⌒

I share this story to emphasize that patience is not putting your head down and meekly enduring a beating given by another. It's not bouncing through life aimlessly either, while being kicked around like a soccer ball on a playing field. It's not putting up with a job for 40 years in the hopes of having a pension at the end of it all. Patience may encompass some misfortune, mistreatment, and hard times for sure - but on the whole the concept of patience is the very opposite of submission to anything. Patience is found in the dogged pursuit of finding your gift or going after a goal, however lofty it might be.

If you are wandering around and having to endure a lot of hard knocks that seem senseless and for nothing, it makes me think that you might not have a larger goal in mind for your life. That's why everything else seems so hard. Not having a life ambition, a driving dream or passion for something tangible, not to be in pursuit of your gifts is what makes life hard. This is one of the driving reasons people leave other destinations and come to America; to pursue a dream and have the freedom to do so. Without an ambition or life goal, it is not patience, it is purposelessness. There is no point in having compass if you're going nowhere.

Patience is endurance, perseverance and steadfastness in the pursuit of a goal. To reach the goal and have the heart to not give up along the way is where these qualities will be most needed. It's determining what gifts God gave you and if you are going to go use them or not. It is knowing where you want to go and then pushing forward by faith to get there. It is a quiet courage. Patience is not so much fighting with others around you, but it is usually face to face encounter with yourself. It's deciding if you like your life and who you are, and if not, what are you going to do about it? It's deep prayerful conversations with God to get the strength you need to pursue the tasks ahead.

May it be so for you and I. May we also have a vision for a good marriage that will be both challenging and life changing for you and your partner; one that will take endurance and focus to achieve. May we find the patience we need to bring the best of ourselves into our marriage. We should therefore, during times of major conflict, have a commitment to each other, being willing to find the patient endurance needed to accomplish this.

And if you feel like you can't make it and you're going to quit, do as my pastor says, "Quit tomorrow, and then postpone it until later."

꒰

Hans Christian Andersen's story of *The Ugly Duckling* illustrates the concept of reflection, or having a proper look at ourselves.

It is the story of an egg that rolled into the wrong nest and resulted in a homely little bird that was attacked by the others around him in the barnyard. He was different but he didn't know why; he just knew that he didn't fit in.

In his plight and frustration he begins to notice how beautiful the swans are. With impossible hopes he wishes he could be like them and be in their company. It would be such a relief from the barnyard he seemed destined to endure and the mockery he had to face daily. It is at some point in the middle of Christian's story that this homely little bird sees his reflection in a pond for the first time. Unforeseen changes had taken place and from the water's surface he sees that he has become, as he desired, a beautiful swan. It was in his eyes a miracle. Overjoyed to leave the mean and critical life of the barnyard behind him, he turns and moves toward the waiting swans placidly moving about the lake.

During any time of separation, our only hope for wholeness is not to attack those around us or relentlessly focus on our spouse's errors. Like the ugly duckling, we need to look deeply into who we are and to see what our reflection is like when it comes back at us. What changes do I need to make? What things have I put off in regards to the marriage I am in? How about my character, my relationship with God, and the use of the gifts that I was given? What kind of reflection do I see now and what do I want to see coming back at me in the future? What problems did I cause and what should I do about them so these actions can be uprooted out of my life for good? During this time of duress, may I suggest that now is the opportune time to leave others out of the picture and take a true look at ourselves.

Be honest and it will pay huge dividends. You want to be a swan and so do I; so also do millions of others around us. It's no accident that *The Ugly Duckling* was Hans Christian Andersen's most revered and best-selling work.

Know that you may never have another unbridled, life changing opportunity to change your future like this one that's before you. Don't just wait idly by, doing nothing different while you wait for your marriage to be mended. Use this chance to enhance who you are, to bring purpose and fulfillment to into your life, and with it, bring more life into your marriage. Take advantage of this time and this problem to see a new you. Maybe what you needed was to see that most of the burden of your unhappiness and the emptiness you felt was not your spouse's fault at all, *but your own*. So place some of the blame and the hope where it belongs – squarely on your shoulders. Take the challenge to begin to find your gifts and expand your horizons. Ask God for His help, for you'll need it.

But also keep the commitment to your spouse while making a different you. It is certainly disheartening to me to see someone who has become a changed person, finding more significance in their life, forsake all of their past associations due to some idea of a newly found self-importance. Remember there is such a thing as character too. It is another attribute that is required to become a great person.

So take your broken wings and learn to fly, but return each evening to the nest you call home. There should never be a conflict over holding your talents, any future fame or fortune, and your marriage in harmony with one another as you go forward.

Our Need For Time Alone

This is so similar to our need for reflection that it may appear redundant – except for one important thing. Reflection can be done with someone present; however time alone is being in a spot where you only have yourself to face. Time alone, and your absence from a bad situation, may be able to accomplish some things in you and your partner's life that you may not be able to see happen in any other way.

- You or your partner may need some time alone to discover how much you really do love each other, and that wrongs that one or both of you have been engaged in will destroy the family you care about and the spouse that you truly love.

- You both may need some time alone to figure out what your roles, responsibilities and priorities are. Hobbies or activities like bowling, car restorations, golf, baseball, computer games, hockey or any other activity should come behind the priority of your relationship. I always advocate that extra time ought to be reserved for searching out and using your gifts first, not spent on play time alone.

- You both may need some time alone to realize that drinking or any other substance abuse is going to kill one of you unless you stop. You may need to know that all your 'secret stuff' isn't so secret at all and everyone knows that you are using. You have most likely become isolated by these choices. You will ultimately end up like you are now, alone, when you drink without concern for others, especially those you love. It may help by isolation to realize that one of you cannot be allowed to destroy your family along with yourself.

-    You both may need some time alone to figure out that physical or emotional abuse is unacceptable. One of you may need to learn that anger or rage will leave you alone in the end anyway because no one wants to be with you if you continue on this path.

-    You or your partner may need some time alone to discover that they need to earn money instead of being idle all the time. They need to find and successfully maintain a job so they can eat. One of you wants them to return as a contributing member of the family and help to pay the bills.

-    You or your partner may need some time alone to discover how much they really need God to replace the areas in their lives where they thought other things, or the other spouse, could fill. You want them to return home as an emotionally and spiritually supportive person instead of being selfish or not concerned for others. Being mature in your faith can take a lot of time, usually years, so set smaller goals initially that will let you know that you both are on your way back to God. It may be church attendance, a bible or devotional study together each night for 15 minutes, or being a part of a home group. Just don't substitute religion for a real spiritual relationship with God and the help of being with others that know him too.

-    You or your partner may need some time alone to discover that these other people they thought were friends are not their friends at all. They need to pick between their associations and their family – if it ever comes to this. They need new and lasting associations, good friends who would support your family, not tear it down.

I must say it's especially tragic to me when a spouse, confronted by separation, misses the boat entirely and uses this opportunity for change to think only of themselves instead. I've seen men and women who have a prime opportunity to prove to their spouse, if they want to, that they still love them and that they're truly willing to make the changes necessary to be together again. Yet instead of doing this they go off and find someone else. They evidently didn't care about the relationship and their spouse's existence with them has been a complete waste of their time.

And know that this time alone has to be organized and communicated well if you want it to be successful. You can meet with a third party and go over the requirements and expectations together in front of them if needed. Realize it can be dangerous or fatal to your relationship if the goals are not clearly understood and the results hoped for are not laid out in a coherent manner. You should want success, so written goals and a structured approach will provide the way to ensure both partners have a clear vision of what's needed so they can reconcile.

It is only loving and fair to be clear with yourself and your partner as to why this is happening, and what you hope the desired objective will be. You will need the support of God and friends to stay accountable to your objectives and not drift off. The goals need to be mutually decided upon – if possible – and not added onto later on if some-thing else comes to mind. That's unfair to keep adding more and more to the list – as it just conveys that you're either pushing your partner away or that the whole issue is really about you. Have friends there or a counselor as needed to make sure you complete your list correctly. There must be a way for the one who has offended to succeed and be restored. Your objective should be to make this possible – not to see them fail. If the goals aren't agreed upon, you will have to reconvene together until everyone understands what is necessary. You should set aside a time, or times, in the near future to review the progress made by one or the both of you.

These are all such important steps. I hope your objectives for your partner are substantial and obtainable, not selfishly motivated or petty. I hope they are truly things of major substance that need renovation and change. You may need the continuing counsel of those you have chosen to make sure you both are on the right track.

Yes, time alone may tell you a lot about your partner and his or her commitment to your relationship. I hope any time absolutely needed to be apart will tell you good things and will only make you hungry to both be back together again.

Our Need to be Responsible

Things had gotten progressively worse to where the relationship was virtually unbearable to Sarah. She had to do something soon and she knew it was going to have to be something drastic.

There were hugs and kisses, soft words together in the beginning, with a lot of cuddling. She liked this and had felt really wanted by him then. There were some learning curves to go through together as time went on, understandably, and some wavering steps to deal with moving forward, just like everyone else she knew. The constant hugging and cuddling had tapered off a bit, but there were still meaningful moments of being together. In those middle years they still found the time to hold each other for a moment and say these words together, "I love you." Their relationship was different, she knew it would be, but she still felt needed and wanted.

But that was so many years ago now and she knew things would never be the same. Their relationship had reached a stage where everything seemingly turned upside down. To Sarah things between them had become very volatile, at times out of control, and she seldom felt safe around him now. He had started to become physically intimidating in ever increasing ways. He bumped her out of the way on occasion when he was coming and she was going in the hallway, and a glaring look from him usually followed their contact. The verbal abuse was a little more intense than the physical contact. In any situation, when confronted with a problem, he would get angry, sullen, and lash out. He had often choose to completely ignore her for days. It all seemed so childish.

He had taken up with some bad associations lately, irresponsibly staying out late at night, and he had begun to drink. She felt there might be women involved too and possible drug use, but she couldn't prove it. He thought she didn't notice when he came in late, but she was aware of it each time. Disturbed and unable to sleep, she could hear the faint creak of the back door opening and shutting in the still of the night. She had begun to find these times were difficult to deal with when he was gone, and that was becoming more and more frequent.

The final straw was when he began to steal things from the house that the family needed, or slip money from her purse when he thought she wouldn't notice. It was all done without regard for her or the others, and all done to support his late night habit of substance abuse and poor associations. When it had come to this point she began to question her role and responsibility in all this. Was she to blame, even partially? She had done the best she could to be a good person and a good example, so she washed herself of any blame. It was all his doing she reasoned and he would have to face the music on his own when the time came.

When it reached this point things went downhill fast. He had lost the respect of several close friends and peers who were good influences in his life. These people, whom she also knew and cared for, came by the house less and less until they didn't come by at all any more. By association, Sarah's reputation had now become tainted. The neighbors had been talking about his goings on and she could sense the faint whispering going behind her back.

She knew what she had to do. It was going to get even uglier for a while, but when things calmed down after his departure she would have peace, stability and safety in her house once more. Sara was going to tell him he had to move out, but she wouldn't take it any further. How could she divorce him? After all, he was her son.

It is interesting and surprising that there is a new movement within this decade to get rid of 'toxic' parents; those who are considered to have been a negative or damaging influence in your life over the years. It is time to set the captives free, some say, and remove the shackles of their bondage from your life for good. There is a process, the divorcement of your parents, or otherwise known as the emancipation of a minor, in which a young person under the age of 18 can legally be recognized as an independent adult. There are also processes in place where the parents can return the favor by legally disowning their children. The New York Times ran an article[1] called 'When Parents Are Too Toxic To Tolerate'. There is also a book called 'Divorcing A Parent'[2], which is a guide to why and how it can be done.

Dr. David M. Allen published an article in Psychology Today[3] that I really liked, in which he questioned this whole course of action. He didn't condone abuse by family members, not at all, but he also didn't think divorcing your family was the only other option. He highlighted that you never really get away from your parents. There are tight bonds between parents and their children that will never be totally diffused and are lodged within our being. These bonds can't be disposed of, avoided or wiped away by the stroke of a pen.

Interestingly, he also indicated that we are modeling damaging behavior and attitudes for our children when we refuse to interact with our own parents. His thought was children that learn the art of disowning one's parents from watching their parents may likely return the favor to them someday.

He felt that you should understand your family history and confront the dysfunction in your family's past. Sure, it is in your parents, but it is also within you or has been handed down to you as well.

There are other options for all of us, whether it is parent to child, child to parent, or parent to parent. It just takes work to dig out the issues and deal with them. It is far more rewarding to fix dysfunctions and brings infinitely better consequences than the other options some suggest. Running away always seems to be a simpler solution, but it is usually the most damaging and irresponsible way to handle things.

⸻

As long as we're on this subject of how to treat those close to us, there are two things that are odd to me regarding divorce. To me they just don't make sense.

One is how quickly some people can fall out of love.

When I have gotten into ended marriage discussions or heard people say things about their divorce, I often will ask them if they still love their spouse. Predictably it catches people off guard. I hear things like,

"Just let me tell you the things he did to me and how he . . . ." I assure them that I get it, but I pursue the unanswered question a bit further by asking again if they still love their spouse.

"Well you don't understand – after all she did? Why she . . . ." and off we go again.

If I can squeeze it in one more time I tell them I understand what they are saying about their previous spouse, but again I'm asking a third time, "*Do you still love them?*" Off they go, ad infinitum, and I seldom get their answer to such a simple question. I am baffled that their love was so conditional upon the other's love being returned. I rarely get an affirmative 'yes' answer to this question.

I reason that there were two people that went to the altar and chances are that at least one of them was truly in love with the other - regardless. Did the person standing before me get married *without* love for their spouse? That sounds like a weird thing to do – get married to someone you don't love. Are they still in love but just don't understand that they are? I think that's a highly possible assumption. I think that love has a life of its own, regardless of how we try to stamp it out. I also think that love and anger might be just different sides of the same postcard. If we didn't love them then their leaving wouldn't make us upset and it wouldn't be an issue.

For example, what if someone came up to me in the store that I didn't know and they said to me, "I never want to have anything to do with you again!" and stomped off. How would I be impacted by this? This unknown person's actions may shock me for a moment, but the whole event certainly won't have a long lasting emotional effect that would keep me up late at night. If someone asks me about the woman in the store, I certainly won't be bitter and angry about it years later or have to give my side of the story for the rest of my life. I wouldn't see myself having to get counseling to get over it. There is no connection between us, this store person and I, and never will be, so I'd let it go.

But if I am upset or angry with someone I've known and been intimate with for a long period of time – that would be different. The emotions I have show that I *really do care for them*. I have a deep connection and there still are feelings for them – you just can't tell it by my actions. The anger or bitterness I show is a sign of a broken love. The love, care and emotions that I feel causes me to say things out of hurt that way down deep inside aren't possibly true at all. As I have said before, there rarely is an amicable divorce where both people are happy with the situation. There is usually one that wanted the other to stay. "Things are not right but yes, I still do love them" is a natural and acceptable reply for a hurt person to admit. It's OK to openly admit this to yourself and then to others. I think it makes you a better human being.

The second oddity to me is the difference in some people's minds between loving their husband and loving their children. There is some kind of confusing dichotomy people strike between the two.

At the start of this story, Sarah cannot bring herself to divorce her son because parents of sound mind *just don't do that*. You can be against your children's actions and not approve of their decisions, and there can be moments of impossibility, but your commitment should always be there for them. I would be sad if it wasn't that way for you. I can't understand moments where you don't want to be around them but I hope you will never abandon your kids.

If we can agree that our children can exhibit the same behavior that counselors would find difficult to condone in a marriage, then why would we keep a son or daughter but abandon a spouse for the same issues? When I ask this question most say that, "It's just different." What? Why? We are all someone's child. I understand that having children come from your own body is an amazing thing – but it is just as profound to men to know that we were involved in it all too. Shouldn't the spouse who brought that child into the world with you be maybe a tad more important than the child? I think so.

I believe that the bond between a husband and a wife, mom and dad, is more intimate. I understand that it is also potentially more volatile than it is with a child, but then again often it is not. With all we have together as adults it seems that our togetherness in life that would be more of a reason to stay. I also know that a healthy marriage, where the kids thrive and feel safe, is where the parents regarded the importance of their relationship above all else, even the kids. So for the sake of the kids and yourselves, during hard times stay together.

⤚

I read about Billy Graham getting ready to speak to a modern woman's movement group. He thought his topic should be on how God has always been for women, to liberate them from oppression, and so forth. When he had the sermon penned out he gave it to Ruth, his wife, to look over and critique as she felt necessary. Ah, Ruth, I wish I had met her. When she gave Billy's sermon back to him later on it was bleeding with red ink. She told Billy it wasn't women's liberation he spoke of, but the liberation of men from their responsibilities that he unknowingly advocated. How true.

Divorce is that same problem in a nutshell. Under the premise of liberating two people from a troubled marriage, it in reality propagates the irresponsibility of many individuals to meet their obligations. Those obligations, in far too many cases, are passed on to others not involved in the form of welfare, social security benefits, unemployment funds and a multitude of social services that will inadequately try to take the place of a father and mother.

And that is what divorce is; a multitude of problems where one parent, or a half of what was once a team, is left to resolve these issues while someone else goes off to another new life. It isn't purely financial, because there are those who pay the bills required, but they still cannot meet the parental requirements they should because they are half of a family, or half of a gender, trying to play both mom and dad when they are only one or the other. And it is raising children who won't see responsibility modeled and quite possibly will think that marriage is a casual affair too. They have no knowledge of what it takes to be married. They haven't seen it – how could they?

I advocate responsibility. It might seem like the hard way to stay committed, or duty for the sake of duty, but the 'easy way' out is fraught with more problems than just doing the correct thing by staying in the marriage.

I personally would rather help in any way I can to see you both succeed. I would like to see you shoulder the responsibility that you together, as parents, were meant to carry.

Lessons to take back to your marriage

1. Treat your spouse as well or better than your kids. If you would never hate or speak evil of your children, give your spouse that brought them into the world along with you the same courtesy.

2. Together, model the marriage that you want your kids, relatives, and those around you in the community to have. Your kids will generally follow the example you set, so be a role model. Those in the community need your marriage for support and encouragement in their lives too.

3. If you're having trouble in your marriage, leave others out of it by leaving someone else's spouse alone. Why would you want to cheat at such a critical time? Secondly, why would you want someone who would cheat and leave their spouse? And for the same reason, why would they want you? These are poor choices and bad trades to make. You're disappointed and things look better 'over there' – I get it - but clear your head. Go get a cup of coffee and talk with a friend. Plan on returning, however difficult, to mowing the grass in your own backyard. No one, regardless of what they say, really likes or respects someone who cheats on their spouse or forsakes their marriage commitment.

Notes

1. When parents are too toxic to tolerate: The New York Times, October 20th, 2009
2. Divorcing a Parent: Beverly Engel, LMFT

Our Need to be Discreet

During this time of separation, know that this should be a private time between you and your spouse, as much as possible.

There may be rumblings and rumors in the community among those in the know, but when approached for more information just ask them to be supportive of your privacy. Zip – that's it. Be clear about the fact that you plan to get back together and that this is just a time of readjustment. Better yet, ask those inquirers to pray for you and your spouse – and leave them with a task.

It will be painful to follow this course of action, it may be a time of tears every now and then when you're alone, but just limit your need for consolation and venting to very close friends. For any hope of success I would strongly admonish you, if that is the right term, to only have conversation and consolation that comes from friends of the same sex as you. Also have it be with those who are committed to your marriage and have your best interests in mind. You never want it to reach your spouse that you are seeing someone of the opposite sex, no matter how innocent, or this whole thing could blow up. You would be considered to be at fault here and labeled possibly for indiscretion and jeopardizing the marriage.

You should hold yourself accountable and never be in this position. Don't be insensitive think a course of action like this, under some assumption of a valid pretense, has any merit. The other person who is thinking of engaging with you should know better too. Please don't be in this situation – even for 1 second.

If you need to be with someone of the opposite sex, make a date to be with your spouse during this time. That is what this whole thing is about anyway.

Our Need for Proper Counseling

I know some folks who have couples in the church they attend with unique but critical situations. In two instances there are husbands who just won't work or attempt to get a job. I don't attend their church but I have met one of the couples.

The gentleman in question is very disarming because his demeanor is overly 'Christian' in nature. What I mean by this is that he appears to be gentle, kind and considerate of all around him in any situation – almost too humble. He certainly caught me off guard when I first met him and began to understand a little bit about his situation. You almost don't want to press him on the obvious subject of work because he appears to be so contrite and friendly. But on the flipside of the coin his wife is working her fingers to the bone. She has to take overtime when she can get it because money is so tight and is exhausted most of the time because she alone has to work to provide for their needs. She keeps food on the table; she keeps a roof over their heads also and she is the only one standing in the gap between them and the street.

I remember one occasion where this topic of work came up and I offered to use my influence to help him get a job. Our large aircraft component factory is usually hiring all the time, and though not all of the jobs are elegant, there is work to be had. I actually did find another man in their church a job where I work – so it wasn't just idle talk. When I pursued this non-working husband about job possibilities his response was,

"Oh, I can't do that because of my back . . ."

"Sorry, I can't do that because it's hard for me to walk . . ."

"I can't . . . . ."

He expertly offered one excuse after another. However, my guess was he could stay at home, walk, sit, move around - evidently well enough to feed himself, take care of his basic needs and possibly relax in front of the TV. Others have offered him work too or have been willing to take him to an unemployment center – but to no avail. Everything is out of his reach or beyond his physical capacity to do, for various reasons. But he'll still smile, be sweet and kind publicly. When these people I knew moved in too close however, he showed a different side. He threatened them, told them not bring anything like this up again and to stay away from speaking to his wife on this issue. Meanwhile his wife is truly acting out being the good Christian wife and suffering under this huge unnecessary load he has created.

So when visiting my friends recently the topic of this man came up again. I told them I was concerned about the marriage of this couple, and if left in this present situation, I could see where it would most likely turn into a divorce. The feelings within this woman, I estimated, were probably churning into a slow boil, like water on the stove getting ready for hot tea or corn on the cob. I envisioned that she would most likely blow-up someday and then the marriage would be over. She would divorce her incompetent husband and possibly also walk away from her faith. It would be probably be evident to her on that day that her friends and the church didn't help, or give her proper counsel, when she needed their support the most. Maybe, in ignorance, all those around her had expected her to carry some pretty heavy burdens that they wouldn't have been willing to carry themselves.

"Why doesn't someone counsel her to ask him to leave the house," I said, "with the stipulation that he must be a wage earning, supportive partner in the marriage before he can return."

"We just don't know what to do," they replied. "We have talked to him over and over, and also suggested that he should go down to the unemployment office and look for some kind of task – but to no avail. We have prayed for them over and over, and are continuing to pray for them."

"In the meantime the water's boiling stronger and the wife needs help and protection," I said. "It's occasions like this where the situation is screaming for help but we don't do the obvious. So this couple eventually gets a divorce – which is clearly not God's will – but all the time separation was a road that could have been taken.

"Which is better," I offered, "having an intervention where he is out, or she is out, until he gets busy joining in the provision of the household, or getting a divorce? What happens if she gets tempted with another man or loses her faith because the church wasn't there to help her when she needed it?"

To me it's like a situation where there is a small fire in the kitchen but we don't get help until the house is finally burning down. I saw some looks round the table when I said this and I wondered if it made sense.

For all the man's excuses, I told my friends that I'd buy a wheel chair and get a cardboard sign so at least this man could make $10.00 or more a day sitting on a corner. He would be helping their situation, and his wife would be encouraged, even if it was in some small way. Through this I had to recognize myself that people who hold a sign up are doing some kind of work and are making some kind of a marginal effort at providing for themselves. It may not be our 9 to 5 job *but they are doing something*. Often times in southern California, when I see someone standing in 90+ degree heat for hours on end, I think that this is harder work than just getting a job.

Are we afraid to communicate this option when divorce is so rampant? Paul at least recognized this option without encouraging it.

I did say before and wholly stand behind it, that separation shouldn't be used for trite, immature or self-serving reasons. If it is used as the next option, the stipulations for returning to the home and to the relationship should be clearly laid out. There should be an obvious task for the partner to accomplish, it should be written down and well thought out. I encourage you to get the counsel and intercession of another solid couple as to what to say and what you're going to write down. You may want their participation also at the meeting that needs to be held so you have some moral support. In all the cautions and careful considerations we should be aware of before pursuing separation, we also shouldn't error on the opposite side by not taking action when it is clearly needed.

When Billy Graham spoke on marriage during the Toronto Canada Crusade on marriage and the family, he said these words,

"There must be a lifetime commitment when you come to Christ. Don't ever entertain the idea of separation and divorce, if you know Christ. He can hold you together. There is no problem you face that cannot be solved by the Lord Jesus Christ.

You say, "Billy, isn't that an idealistic picture?" Of course it is, but it is a picture of what everyone is looking for in marriage; love and joy and peace and happiness. And I don't know how anyone can pursue it without the grace and the power of God today."

We shouldn't separate with the intent of splitting up. Being apart is more difficult than staying together, for the most part. If there are going to be times apart, they need to be as short as possible and structured. In whatever we do, the goal is to save the marriage.

⟜

If you are considering getting help, be it a marriage & family counselor or a personal counselor, you should know a few things.

First of all, the traditional route of seeing a marriage counselor, especially a good one, can be costly. Maybe you're in a place where the cost is prohibitively expensive and you'd like to know what your options are. The expense of a professional is certainly cheaper than divorce and the legal dissolution of the marriage for sure, but it won't feel like it at the time. Thankfully many of the good ones offer some kind of a sliding scale based upon what your income is like.

Secondly, before seeing a particular counselor, I would have an interview with the one I choose before putting down money. It's not really the money at this point; I would just need to know what they believe. If I'm intelligent and aware, I need to recognize that I have my wife, my family and my future that I'm going to put into their hands. I'm asking guidance on what is the second most important thing in life, God being first. If we're going to open our lives up to them, I would consider it a fair trade if they opened up about their lives to us before we start. If they won't allow an introductory time to discuss who they are, what values they adhere to and how they run their practice, whether it happens over the phone or in their office, I would steer away.

In that introduction I would need to know,

a. Are they committed to marriage? They are a *marriage and family counselor*, right? I want to know what they believe when they see someone whose back is up against the wall. I would also want to know if they would ever advocate a divorce and why.

b. Would they ever counsel for divorce unless it is for infidelity – and even then with caution? You would be surprised how many of them would counsel for divorce in various tough, but non-infidelity situations. That's partially why I'm writing this book. Maybe it's what they were taught in school – I don't know – but you *need* to know.

c. How do they feel about separation in tough times, to keep the family together, vs. divorce? This may be new to them but must be discussed.

d. If they allowed you to follow them home, what is their family situation like? What strengths do they bring into counseling from their own marriages and what things are they working on? This is very important, more important than you think. Just because you went to college to be an architect it doesn't mean that your house is clean and beautiful. Because you are an accountant it doesn't mean that your bills or financial life is in order. Just because you're an engineer it doesn't mean that you can fix everything in your home. You've heard about the plumber's wife who struggles with the drainage in her sinks and getting a decent kitchen at home? Same here. Just because they went to college and have a psychology or marriage practice license on the wall doesn't mean that they have a good marriage. Sorry, it just doesn't, and you can't assume that it does. It's fair to ask if they can share a bit on where they are at in their marriage.

I should say that I am not against professionals; however there is also another very effective option – depending on your situation. Some of the best counselors that life has to offer are free – of no real charge – except your commitment to the time that they'll spend with you and maybe the cost of a cup of coffee. Long before there were professional counselors there was another way. How often this is ignored!

The Apostle Paul writes,

'Teach the **older men** to exercise self-control, **to be worthy of respect,** and to live wisely. The must have sound faith and be filled with love and patience.

Similarly, teach the **older women** to live in a way that honors God. They must not slander others or be heavy drinkers. Instead, they should teach others what is good. **These older women must train the younger women** to love their husbands and their children, to live wisely and be pure, to work in their homes, to do good, and to be submissive to their husbands. Then they will not bring shame on the word of God.

In the same way, encourage the young men to live wisely. **And you yourself must be an example to them** by doing good works of every kind. Let everything you do reflect the integrity and seriousness of your teaching. Teach the truth so that your teaching can't be criticized. Then those who oppose us will be ashamed and have nothing bad to say about us.'[1]

The whole concept of the early church, spelled out in many of his letters, was for responsible people with good lives to be approachable and touchable examples in the church. Paul knew he wasn't going to always be around; he had many people and places to see so he wanted to leave behind role models that could provide solid, practical leadership for the lives of those he had fought so hard to win. In Paul's thinking, it had nothing to do with seminary or doctorate degrees. They were to be every day husbands and wives, single people also, that were of good character and available to others. They were not to be on the shelf like a museum piece that you can only see through glass, but people you could talk to and be with on a personal level. They were to be touchable and open to examination. They were to be people who gave good advice because they lived out on a personal level what they believed. It is the same criteria for them that I ask for from a professional too; all but the credentials.

God's plan for this was all for a purpose. The church was to be a model, on a smaller scale, of how society should be and act.

Our marriages are to be a small example of the perfect church – showing how Christ (the husband) treats us and how we (his bride) treat Him. Is that where we are today? Because we have missed the mark in many ways is the same reason why it's tough to see the Christian faith in the place we see today.

You don't know how many times I've gotten poor advice at the church level and wondered how someone came up with that type of counsel. Almost every time I would find out, then or later, that they were just reflecting what they had done with their own lives – marrying several times, divorcing for selfish or impure reasons, or whatever. How can you legitimately tell someone else it's wrong to live a certain way, when you're doing the same thing? Or how do you admit your second marriage is wrong when your new husband is standing by or within earshot? People won't because they don't want a second divorce when their spouse hears their comment. In the same way, you wouldn't ask a single person to counsel on marriage would you? They haven't lived it out and don't understand the dynamics it requires on a daily basis. I have serious questions, therefore, on the wisdom of a priest or a Pope to dole out advice on marriage when they know nothing personally about it. They should not take this role to themselves but be guides to send you to someone within the church, or at the professional level, who can properly speak to these issues.

You should notice however, sooner or later, that you are surrounded by people around you that are living balanced, well rounded lives. Sometimes their existence is one of the reasons your situation seems to be a mess, like a shadow that darkens your lives. You can't avoid sticking out like a sore thumb because you are around some people that are living out their lives with at least reasonable success. Believe it or not, some of them would be honored to help you at least be where they are at. The only key is you have to reach out and ask them.

We kind of do this informally at times when we get insight from others when we meet for coffee or dinner together, but this is a more formal request to spend time alone with a couple you respect. Know it should be both of them together with both of you. If one or the other of them doesn't have time or can't be a part of this effort, then move on to another couple who will both be present. It's so important to get the wife's perspective on the husband and their marriage, and vice versa. It keeps the couple you meet with honest, rather than one of them alone saying they are the greatest when reality is really far different.

The only time you will meet together separately is if the guy wants to meet alone with your husband, or the wife wants to meet alone with your wife. Anything cross gender is off limits and should never be suggested or hinted at. All of this should be decided ahead of time when, as a group, you're going over how your meetings will be.

Because of this approach, I would suggest that you find a couple that you may normally feel slightly or massively uncomfortable to approach because maybe you think they have a perfect life. Ask them if they would consider giving you both some insights into having a better marriage, from their perspective. If they shy away or are not open to this, unless for a good reason, then I would suspect that they are not as perfect or as open to examination on a personal level as you might think. Anyone who has had trouble and worked through it successfully knows how important it is to get good help. Because of what they've experienced, or because they are just good people who understand their role in the church, they hopefully would be available to help you at some level. You'll be surprised how many couples would love to be asked. You may also be surprised as to how many great marriages were on the shaky ground at one time or another, but found a way to blossom and bloom. If one couple doesn't have all the answers – don't be afraid to reach out to more couples as you go along. You may have a lifetime experience of reaching out to others, just to enrich your lives, or you may become asked at some point to help someone else. Just be honest about who you are and ask for privacy about what you share.

The nice part about this type of approach is you can see what you're getting in advance. Going to a professional doesn't mean that you get to follow them home. As I've said before, just because someone has a sheepskin on the wall doesn't mean that they have a marriage themselves that is worth emulating. In this case you have a chance to 'interview' the couples you might choose first hand or slightly from afar, by reviewing who they are before you approach any of them. You can look at their kids, look at how they get along when they think no one is noticing, how he treats her, how she treats him, how they both treat the kids, whether he still opens the car door for her, how clean they are, how well do they take care of their things, how they talk together when alone in a crowded room, and so much more. Take your time to observe them before you ask, unless you already know something about them from church or where you socialize.

Don't be afraid to be uncomfortable with who you might choose – you are looking to go to a higher level. And don't be afraid to choose someone who is ahead of you by 10 or more years. It's sad when the wisdom of older people, and all they can offer, is passed by.

Two rules here. Realize that what you talk about, on both sides, is personal and should not be repeated outside of the walls where you meet. Secondly, don't be surprised or shocked if they're not perfect. God doesn't ask people to be perfect, but only to strive to be better than they are today. The Gospel, the Good News, isn't about our lives but His. I don't want a perfect you; it would put me off. I just want a good you who is approachable.

The point I am trying to make is get real help – whether a professional or a lay person. I just think that real help has to be real help though, and it has to be clearly identified as being just that. I admonish you up front that associations during your time of hardship are critical and can be another type of 'counseling' that you may not be aware of. I would avoid those who are divorced or have left a marriage to get remarried again. It's not that they are bad people; I've just found that people give advice based upon how they have lived their lives vs. what they may often know to be true but haven't followed. It can be disastrous to hang out with those that would undermine your marriage or tell you that the grass is greener somewhere else. You have to be selective and isolate both of yourselves from poor advice – regardless of how much these people are your 'friends'. Real friends will want your best, not for your marriage to dissolve. Real friends may tell you things that you need to hear, not what you want to hear.

I know that many couples are desperate and they don't have time and money to waste on dead ends. This is why I am so in favor of finding someone with the kind of life you can see first-hand for yourselves; a life that you want for the both of you, a marriage that works, and an example to follow. Sometimes they may already know about you as well and may be praying for you. Maybe they will approach you first – we should all be so blessed. Maybe they will be a professional that comes highly recommended. Maybe your church or your pastor knows of a good professional. Maybe your friends have been helped greatly and they have someone they can recommend. And maybe someone who knows you or that you meet with will give you some funds to go where you couldn't normally afford to go. Maybe the professional will offer some kind of discount. I don't know, but all of these options may be available to you.

Either way, in any way, don't be shy. Getting the help you need, regardless of whether it's professional or not, is of the essence. Just make sure it's good help.

It's interesting that I ran into a gentleman who talked about how his church was successfully growing.

"How are you doing this?" I asked, hoping to learn something.

"Well," he said, "we don't expect new comers to be perfect. It's not about perfection anyway, it's about the journey. They are going to come with problems and we are prepared to meet them on their level, where they are at. The exciting part is starting from where you're at and beginning to see growth. We expect them to be babies in the faith and we also expect to clean up many messy diapers.

We just don't ask them to meet our standards or be where we are at. Churches that don't grow are the ones that have a lot of people with head knowledge that expect perfection. They can't deal with real people or real issues. It puts people off when they are looked down upon until they reach a certain level or place of growth."

I think this illustrates another caution I have that centers around reading marriage advice books.

First know that there are some great marriage books out there. I personally have immensely enjoyed and benefited from Gary Chapman's book 'Things I Wish I'd Known Before We Got Married'. He has written this on a very personal and practical level, sharing what he has learned in his own life and marriage. His understanding of what forgiveness is has been the single best writing on the subject I have ever found.

Secondly, however, know that marriage books can set-up some unrealistic expectations. It's like the church growth information I got above. Do I come at my marriage knowing that it's OK to start flawed? Can I start where I'm at and be happy with the growth I achieve? A lot of these books just seem to paint a perfect relationship when they should equally stress that you should be happy with any growth forward that you can obtain, regardless if it's perfect or not. I'm not advocating that anyone should 'settle for' mediocrity, but I am also not setting you up to abandon ship if you aren't achieving the ideals that are given in some of these books. Lastly, I wish more of these books would ask us to what levels are we willing to go to if everything isn't perfect? Are we willing, for the sake of integrity and the family, to live out 'for better or for worse'? What advice do they present on how to do this?

I know we want to lead people to greener pastures, and I agree with this, but what do we offer if those pastures are not readily, if ever, attainable? It's not fair to remain silent on this subject and just paint a fairy tale existence. I would rather paint a realistic picture of some struggles and imperfections in the one you love while you are both on a journey through life that is ultimately worthwhile.

Notes

1. Paul on how regular people can help in the church: The New Testament, Titus 2:2-8 [NLT]

Our Need to Choose New Associations

"Associate yourself with people of good quality, for it is better to be alone than in bad company."

Booker T. Washington

Friends and Companions

'I will be careful to live a blameless life . . . . I hate all who deal crookedly; I will have nothing to do with them.

I will search for faithful people to be my companions. Only those who are above reproach will be allowed to serve me. I will not allow deceivers to serve in my house, and liars will not stay in my presence.'

Psalms 101:3 - 7
NLT – New Living Translation

Our Need to Choose New Associations

It's interesting that in the Psalms, written by King David, it deals right away in the first Psalm with who you associate with and how it will affect your life. You would think the first thing David would say might be regarding something else a bit more important or profound, but no. Evidentially the King found it profound and enough of a critical issue that associations needed to be discussed up front. He therefore begins to talk with us about our companions and asks us to consider the wrong and the right choices regarding them.

He writes,

> 'Blessed is the man who walks not in the counsel of the ungodly, nor stands in the path of sinners, nor sits in the seat of scoffers.'[1]

In the Book of Proverbs that follows the Psalms, written by David's son Solomon, it's interesting to me that this same theme pops up at the very beginning as well.

> 'My son, hear the instruction of your father, and do not forsake the teaching of your mother; for they will be a garland of grace on your head, and chains about your neck. My son, if sinners entice you, do not consent. If they say, "Come with us, let us lie in wait for blood,

let us lurk secretly for the innocent without cause; let us swallow them up alive as the grave, and whole, as those who go down into the pit; we will find all kinds of precious possessions, we will fill our houses with spoil; cast in your lot among is, let us all have one purse: My son, do not walk in the way with them, keep your foot from their path.'[2]

When my relationship with my wife was in trouble, the first thing that began to impress itself upon me was the importance of who would I choose for my friends and associates? Who was I going to have around me? Would they be helpful? Would they encourage me to faithfulness, or would they ask me to abandon my hopes of having someone who meant so much to me come back? It was difficult at times. I had my close friend who was at my wedding tell me upfront that I was spinning my wheels, that I just didn't get it, and that I should move on. Maybe that was the way it was going to turn out anyway, but no one knew for sure at that time. I look back and I don't think this was good advice then or now – for you should always fight for your marriage and your family - regardless. But, it was an introduction to the fact that the journey was going to be tough enough without the 'help' of bad counsel.

At such a critical time I am thankful that it became readily apparent to me as to who was for my marriage and who was not. I stayed around those who were committed to me staying faithful to my marriage. Outside of all the other things that happened, my decision as to whom I associated and surrounded myself with, and who I did not, made the largest, single difference in how my circumstances turned out. No wonder David and Solomon made this issue so prominent at the beginning of their writings.

If you feel that your marriage is in trouble, or if you're currently separated, begin to take a look at the people in your life. Who is there for you, supporting you in the right direction when you count close friends, and who should not be there? Who should you be with and how can you get the right kind of people into your life? There are some that you may need to ween out of your inner circle for the time being, and those that you may need to separate yourself from altogether. At the same time there are some good people you haven't met yet and those you know *of* but haven't gotten to know them *well enough* yet. You will need to cultivate a closer relationship with good people like this.

During this time of finding the associations that I needed, it was odd to me to find out that the church was not as safe a place I thought it was. I don't mean that the church where I worshiped in was in a bad neighborhood or full of dangerous people, but within its confines were some folks with very poor advice. Almost always, upon further examination, I found that they were usually people who had made these same poor decisions themselves. I was in church, which most often is a good environment, so I expected to find the best of the best in counsel there. Instead I found some who would say 'move on' or 'you'll do better next time.' What? I may not have noticed this under normal circumstances but it was especially impactful to me then because it was a hurtful and discouraging time where I was trying to get my family back.

When King David said to 'walk not in the counsel of the ungodly' I just didn't realize he may have meant that I would have to be on-guard in my own church, in the place where I thought I could feel the safest. I later realized that he went through an experience like this that was similar to mine.

He wrote,

'For it is not an enemy that who reproaches me; then I could bear it. Nor is it one who hates me, who has exalted himself against me; then I could hide from him. **But it was you, my peer, my guide, and my**

acquaintance. We took pleasant counsel together, and walked to the house of God in company.'[3]

David was blind sighted by those that he didn't expect to have to be on guard with. He was surprised by a close friend who should have stayed a close friend, but did not. I say all this to emphasize that you will have to make some selective choices if you are going to get the sense of direction and encouragement that you need, even at your church.

There were great examples also, thankfully. I found married couples within those hallowed walls who were on course – even some who had recovered from some tough situations – young couples as well as old. They were there for the picking all along and I never knew to even ask! I had always been able to see their lives at close range but I never had the confidence to ask them for their help. You want to get to know couples who live out the right principles and are willing to come along side you to help restore your marriage in any way they can. Just know that a lot of them would be flattered if you asked. I wish you the best on your journey – just know that you weren't meant to do it alone. I hope that someone comes along your way to provide the encouragement that you need. I know that they're there – God knows to – He just wants to help you in this way also.

One more practical piece to add to this – if you're a guy, stay with the guys or get help from families that are intact or healthy. If you're a gal, stay with the gals or associate yourself with families that you'd be safe with. You partner needs to see that you're going to be faithful while you're apart or they'll never want to get back together with you again.

It is so sad to me personally to see some on dating sites with the description of 'currently separated' next to their names. At a time when they should be slowing down and considering their marriage, they are out there already looking again and moving away from their current commitment. They are playing fast and loose in my opinion.

Maybe you think that this is OK, that they look terrific and that they might be a fantastic future partner – but I think this kind of person is a poor choice. If their commitment is so shallow to the situation they are in, if they can't even wait for the ink to dry before they're out trying to find someone else, do you think that they wouldn't do the same thing to you? Do you think that you're special?

So stay faithful – don't cheap out on the future, yourself, or your character. Commit your ways to the one you love.

Notes

1. King David on choosing our companions wisely: The Old Testament – Psalm 1:1 [Modern English Version - MEV]
2. Solomon on choosing our companions wisely: The Old Testament – Proverbs 1:8 – 15 [MEV]
3. Being on guard in your place of worship: The Old Testament – Psalms 55:12 – 14 [MEV]

Our Gifts

"I'm a firm believer in the theory that people only do their best at the things they truly enjoy."

Jack Nicklaus

Our Gifts

"The meaning of life is to find your gift. The purpose of life is to give it away."

Pablo Picasso

Our Need to Find Our Gifts

Overlooking the ocean in San Diego is a place that is one of my favorite spots. It's a little park with a grassy area, open to all, that is nestled in an expensive neighborhood. The locals have known about it for years and several of the park benches have memorial placards on them to those who spent years at this spot. I was fortunate to meet one of them before he left this life, never to return to his bench near the sea again. I have often found moments of solace there, either being alone or with just a few people, watching the waves, the surfers, looking at the vastness of nature and the sweeping expanse of the ocean.

During one of these late afternoons a motorhome pulled up and three young people got out. What looked to be a couple and a solo friend turned out to be 3 siblings from Argentina on a tour of the California coast. One of my gifts is the ability to interact with total strangers and secondly, if possible, have them open up to me on more than just surface level. We talked about their lives, their parents, what they hoped to see on their short visit and a bit about their Catholic faith. It was about a 2 hour visit that we had together and I thoroughly enjoyed talking to them.

There were many interesting things I learned about their family, their lives and their country, but what impacted me the most was a few words at the end with the oldest brother. He was a career counselor in Buenos Aires and his main goal was to help people get into productive careers but also get them to think about their giftedness.

"People often go after the wrong things," he told me. "They go after material objects. They try to get an exotic car of some sort, or an expensive watch, fine clothes, a large house and a host of other things – thinking that this will make them feel important and also fulfill their deepest needs. But it doesn't happen that way. Instead we should pursue finding our God given gifts and use them to bring meaning and happiness into our lives, and to be of help to others. You may get the expensive car after that, or you may not, but you will have the happiness you desire and find your eventual purpose in life. Finding and using your gifts will always be more valuable and satisfying than money or things."

In the end I gave them some places to see and directions on how to get there from where we were standing – not really a huge deal. Looking back I feel that our transaction wasn't evenly meted out. Not only did I get the gift of their presence for a while, but I was also given guidance on how to set a different course for my life and find purpose for the days I have left. Did God give me a gift that is uniquely mine? I had find out. Did He do this for me so I could be great and famous, or was His purpose for these gifts so I could be useful in helping others? What were the ramifications of ignoring these gifts? Maybe it was the reason for much of the emptiness I had been experiencing in my life, up until now. I set about trying to find out which gifts were mine.

I found that there are several places where can get tripped up on the pursuit of finding your God given gifts.

One is to want the gifts of another.

For years I wanted to play golf like Jack Nicklaus, Paul Azinger, Tiger Woods, Ricky Fowler and the like – I even begged God for this. But in the end I didn't have the same kind skill or golfing talent. But I practiced, and practiced some more, and even built a hitting net in our backyard. However, the more I played it seemed the worse I got. Golf wasn't my purpose for life but I couldn't see this initially, and when I did see it I fought it.

In contrast, think of Nick Faldo, who won the British Open and a few Masters Tournaments over his great career. In 1971 he was watching Jack Nicklaus win the Masters on TV and decided then and there that golf was what he wanted to do. A scant 6 years later he was not only playing professionally but played Jack and his American teammate in the international competition called the Ryder's Cup. Along with his teammate, he won his match against them. That is a rare thing when you consider the talent he was playing against.

It is amazing to realize that some of the *exceptionally* gifted can have personal handicaps in their lives and still outperform the regulars. Imagine Joe Namath, the very talented New York football quarterback, who smoked cigarettes on the sidelines between plays but still was above his peers on the field. Imagine professional baseball players, those who make a living at it, stopping what they were doing during warm-ups just to see Mickey Mantle hit in the batting cage. Toward the end of his life, with a legendary career already in the books, Mickey regretted how he had squandered his God given talents by living life in the fast lane off of the field. The professionals who envied him, then and today, would take his career of achievements in a minute. But he said he could have been better. Things like this are hard to imagine.

Some have these extra extraordinary gifts and some don't – but we all have gifts. I'm not saying it doesn't take work even for the extra ordinary, but our gifts, however little or great, will be evident to all if we use them.

Secondly, many waste their time on frivolous pursuits and never get on with life.

What a shame it is to be staring at your smart phone for years on end when you could be out finding and enjoying your talents. It will make a tremendous difference in your emotional, physical and financial future to find who you were meant to be – but you're staring at a screen playing games or texting instead of becoming the real you. Put the phone down and begin your life! Others get consumed in hobbies or extra-curricular sports activities like I did – imagining they are Mickey Mantle, Michael Jordan or

Dale Earnhardt. Remember that hobbies and sports aren't bad, but they can also be the enemy of our finding the best direction for our future.

Thirdly, some don't know or believe that having gifts applies to them.

They think there was no purpose for them coming into this world and they live their life accordingly. Maybe no one has ever believed in them or they have never met someone like my friend from Argentina. I'm a firm believer that all of us have gifts. God didn't cheat you or anybody else – you just have to search them out.

Maybe the last thing is we just don't know how to find them.

The most practical guidance I found comes from the Proverbs of Solomon.

> "Sow your seed in the morning, and at evening let your hands not be idle, **for you do not know which will succeed, whether this or that, or whether both will do equally well.**"[1]

You have to begin trying things, some already of interest to you and some you may have not even explored yet. It is only by beginning the journey that you will eventually find your way. If your gift ultimately helps your self-esteem, realize that it also helps your marriage. Your spouse will know how to support you constructively if you are a thriving individual with a sense of direction for the future.

You have gifts and they are uniquely yours, I just hope you have the passion to find them, and through them, find the purpose for your life.

Since they are God given gifts it may help to ask for His guidance – but maybe that's just me talking. I don't think it could hurt.

Notes

1. Working to find our gifts / Solomon: The Old Testament – Ecclesiastes, chapter 11:6 [NIV]

Our Need to Find God

I have a good friend of mine in the professional world who gave me a valuable tool for my life. I was in what appeared to be a permanent funk due to life circumstances, and in that place of grey scenery and daily monotony, he told me to go make memories. Take a camera, go places that you haven't been before, try things that you've put off and enjoy life in a different way. He wasn't implying anything reckless or immoral, but to just explore the beautiful and search out the unknown.

The first 'push off from the dock' came unexpectedly from my brother Bryan. I was working in Seattle and we were close to each other again after being so long apart. We had such wonderful times making up for lost opportunities due to jobs putting us in different states. As we spent time together I didn't notice that I had been discussing motorcycles a lot, but he picked up on it. While sitting over Chinese food in Seattle's International District, Bryan said, "Look man – you talk about it all the time – why not go do it? You're going to be 70 years old before you know it and then it will be too late." His words stuck in my head for months and I couldn't dislodge them. Before too long I decided to take action. It felt ridiculous to me that in my mid to late 50's I was going to be so reckless as to get on a motorcycle. Now, 6 or 7 motorcycles later, it has been something that I've thoroughly enjoyed. When I'm alone, which is a lot, and I need to get out, I saddle up, feel the wind in my face and go. It's called 'wind therapy.'

Since moving back to San Diego after so many years, I wasn't sure that there was much to see or many destinations to pursue.

I wasn't looking forward to just making trips to the local tourist spots, so I joined up with some guys from work to venture out to new places. One of the guys, however, wasn't going to get out of bed any earlier than 9:00am on a Saturday, because it was his day to relax after a long work week. It felt like noon before we usually got started and half the day seemed wasted. What seemed like an obstacle turned out to be a blessing in disguise.

As I parted a bit from that group, I began to think of the various places I'd been but began to wonder what they would look like at a different time of the day. So I went to the Coronado Beach like usual, but I went at 4:00am in the morning. Seeing the great hotel and beach go from early morning darkness to dawn was very memorable. The next trip was out to Pt. Loma for the evening, to sit on the site of the Veteran's Memorial and watch the sun go down while overlooking the cliffs and the ocean. That also was very memorable – so I was two for two. Just recently I went out to the little mountain town of Julian for a night ride and had the chance to walk the streets at 9:30pm, after they rolled the sidewalks up. I was virtually alone. I saw the lights of the Julian Hotel and made a mental note to bring a loved one there some time in the future, if that was to be, for a special anniversary. But the most incredible part of that ride was leaving Julian, soon after walking the town, and coming through the Laguna Mountain area, via the Sunrise Highway, at 11:00pm at night.

While in the US Navy years ago I had made the discovery that the stars virtually disappeared when they were in competition with city lights. We were out in the Indian Ocean on one of our travels and the stars were so thick above that there was more star light than dark that night. The deep blackness above was in submission to all the twinkling lights and large bands of the Milky Way within it. Weeks later when we came into Singapore for leave and refueling, all of those stars disappeared due to the city's electrical brightness. Years had passed and I had never again seen stars like I had that night in the Indian Ocean – it was just a memory. But it all came back on the Sunrise Highway in California at 11:00pm that night.

It was totally unexpected and breathtaking. I had pulled over at the place where there was an observation deck that overlooks the desert valley below and shut off my motorcycle. A nearby camper and his wife came down on impulse, just like I had, and we found ourselves together under this amazing light show of the stars above [thank you Kyle and Hanna – I enjoyed it]. I thought several lights were planes overhead because they twinkled so bright that they looked like aircraft heading in and out of the San Diego airport, way down in the city. But they were stars after all, twinkling brightly. Standing there in the darkness, I found the only way I could take it in was in sections. So tried to piece it together by turning around and around but it was still beyond my total comprehension. I reflected that night that I hadn't seen the Big Dipper for years, but there it was, faithfully in the sky where I'd left it as a child.

⌒

When God led Abraham outside of his tent on such a dark night as I was experiencing, He asked Abraham to look up. Without any distracting city lights to mute out the sky in his day, God told Abraham his descendants were going to be as numerous as the stars overhead. To many of us city dwellers that statement doesn't make any sense. The Bible seems irrelevant because Abraham must have had more descendants than just the 3 to 6 correlating stars that I see overhead when standing on my porch in my neighborhood. But go out a long ways, far away from the bustle of life, and you'll see things much differently.

In the same way we need a quiet spot, similar to what I'm describing above, to think everything out. It is good to ponder our lives and seek a better understanding of who God is. We need friends and church too, but we also need time to contemplate alone, so our faith can be produced in isolation too. The convictions we need for life often have to be developed just between ourselves and Him, in times when no one else is around.

∽

I learned that it is true when the Bible says the heavens above us declare the glory of God and that the earth is filled with His glory. You just have to be in the right spot, both physically, mentally and heart wise to see it. Can you imagine the cosmonauts in space that said, "We're out here, but we don't see any God." That's a clear example of the right location, the wrong mentality and a darkened heart.

God's reflection is in the ocean, in the simplicity of children, in all the plants and animals around us too, but nothing is quite like this canopy of light overhead, sitting above us on a dark, clear night.

It is my hope that you can find Him and find Jesus at the same time. If you didn't come into your marriage knowing Him, I am of the opinion that you will certainly need Him now. God sent Jesus from beyond the galaxies to earth into human history to make sure you could find Him. As I said before, His coming wasn't done in a corner but historically out in the open for all mankind to see.

One of my favorite verses of how we should begin the journey to get to know Him is expressed in a story Jesus told of two people in a dispute, on their way to court.

Jesus relates it to us in this way,

"When you are on the way to court with your adversary, settle your differences quickly. Otherwise, your accuser may hand you over to the judge, who will hand you over to an officer, and you will be thrown into prison. And if that happens, you surely won't be free again until you have paid the last penny."[1]

Settling matters quickly means we have time to work things out now if we just don't keep putting it off, and off, and off - until another day. Don't wait until someone shows up at your door with some religious solution that may not be the right thing for you eternally. It may be difficult to start finding God but try finding a good church to attend. Ask a few people at work that you know and trust where they congregate on Sunday. When you can, pray in the best way you know how and ask God for His help on your journey. Stay away from any deception or religious offshoots that have a fight to pick with normal Christianity and you'll do well. I don't want to see you go from the pan into the fire so to speak.

But the admonition Jesus gives is to not wait until death takes you away; for once you're gone from this world you're out of opportunities to make things right. Before the only rightful Judge of all mankind, you will find that there is no more time left to make a choice on your faith or reconcile on what you put off. You had time; you just didn't take the time or make room for Him in your busy, daily life.

If you're reading this you still have time – please make the best use of it.

Notes

1. Settling matters while we have time: The New Testament – Matthew, chapter 5:25-26 [NLT]

CHAPTER **10**

On Divorce

Divorce

'People ruin their lives by their own foolishness and then are angry at the Lord.'

Proverbs 19:3
New Living Translation

A Path of Hurt

'When people fall down, don't they get up again?
When they discover they're on the wrong road, don't they turn back?
Then why do these people stay on their self-destructive path? . . .

They cling tightly to their lies, and will not turn around.
I listen to their conversations and don't hear a word of truth.
Is anyone sorry for doing wrong?
Does anyone say, "What a terrible thing I have done?"
No! All are running down the path of sin as swiftly as a horse galloping into battle . . .
They do not know the Lord's laws.'

Jeremiah 8:4-7

NLT

Divorce

Is divorce an option?

There has probably been a lot of hurt that has taken place if you're in this spot. It is a place I believe that you shouldn't be in. But if there hasn't been adultery and you're willing to stay in this position, all is still redeemable. You say, "Oh well, I am already divorced, so it's too late." This is not true. Unless you or your spouse has made the unwise choice of getting married again, the doors are still open for reconciliation.

As you know by now, divorce is a bad road to go down. It will affect a larger circle of friends, more than just your immediate family, in probably a hurtful way. In almost 100% of the instances it has a bad outcome for all involved. It was a chain of unwise thinking in almost all cases that got you here and only a change in your thinking will get you out. Think deeply about it before you continue on this path. It may hurt you emotionally to stay in your marriage more than others may know, but please avoid dissolving the marriage for good if at all possible. As I've mentioned, separation is a viable option that gives you the space to be apart, it stops the hurt, but more importantly it avoids unraveling a good thing. Separation avoids further hurt by keeping lawyers and the court system from getting involved – those who may have the sole purpose in mind of accomplishing the dissolving your marriage.

Four things I can say about this last choice of divorce.

First, any two people that get to this place are definitely in trouble or at the very least having the most severe argument that they can have. Secondly, there is a problem and at least one of you thinks that it was unsolvable. Thirdly, for every person who wants out of a marriage there is generally one person who wants them to stay in. And finally, if there are children involved they are going to get hurt, often for life. The pain is not going to just go away or get easier with time.

There is a pretty consistent pattern laid out that at least one of the two persons has to go through. It is a 3 step process and it looks like this:

a. One person has make it official that they want to get a divorce and they are leaving the marriage.

b. That same person has to see a lawyer to dissolve the marriage in court through a written, legal document that needs to be signed, ideally, by the both of you. The other person doesn't have to sign it, but if they don't, it will be delivered to them personally by a courier. What a job that must be to have.

c. Finally, the person that has gone through a & b above has to either ask you to move your belongings out of the home you share, or they take theirs and leave.

This same process above, in a slightly different sequence, is written out in Deuteronomy 24:1.

'Suppose a man marries a woman but she does not please him. Having discovered something wrong with her, he writes a document of divorce, hands it to her, and sends her away from his house.'

I believe it is good to go through this 3 step process, for at each step you have an opportunity to reconsider what you are doing. If you don't reconsider, you have a hurdle to jump over

3 times that only a person whose heart has hardened against the relationship can do.

⌇

Just remember that divorce is not the end people say it is. It is my hope that neither of you continue to go this direction without turning around. In most all cases it is a poor choice to make, but depending on the choices you make *afterwards* it is redeemable.

So in this regard I don't want to leave you without hope. I want to tell you the story of two people that did divorce but found a way to come back together. They turned it around, but it only happened after they saw the bigger picture.

Are they heroes in their community, like those who are honored in parades? I think they should be. At the very least they are heroes to me.

In this one last chapter, let me tell you the story about their life.

Craig, Jill and Hunter

There is a couple from my home town in Idaho that fell in love and began their married life together with reasonably high expectations. A first child named Jessie came into their world and a second, Hunter, followed soon after. All went well with their family and their marriage until Jesse, at age 10, was diagnosed with leukemia. I can't imagine what it would have been like for me or you, at this age, to have been so young and probably so unprepared for this kind of event in our lives.

As a well-known couple in the community, when the news arrived of Jesse's condition, a lot of folks pulled together as one to help them in any way they could. I'm sure it happens in the city too, but having been in a small town at one point in my life, this aspect of pulling together is especially associated in my thinking to small, tight knit communities. Maybe it's because it is more visible there than it would be in a large city. Their pastor and many close friends came along side Craig and Jill, doing practical things - as well as being there to listen, to pray with them when gathered together and to pray for them when they were not around.

With Jesse, as it also was with the family, it was a roller coaster ride. For the 22 months that he lived with this disease, his family endured stresses that few can imagine. Jesse would get better, and then things would go back to bad again. He went to Seattle for treatment, receiving a bone marrow transplant, and the situation turned for the better. But the joy and hope was only to last for a while. Eventually Jesse succumbed, passing away at the young age of eleven and the entire community mourned his departure.

It must have been unbelievably hard to talk with your son during his time of his sickness, looking into those young eyes and hoping you could say and do the right things. Craig and Jill are amazing people but I'm sure they didn't feel up to the task many times – and I imagine none of us would have felt adequate either. While talking with them on an August evening, Jill reflected on Jesse asking her at one point if he would die. What do you say? She told me that the doctors encouraged them both not to lie to their child during these important hours of his life. I think that was wise. So she told Jesse, "Yes buddy, you are." Jill is an amazing lady to the core and formidable when she has to be.

I think of Peter Marshall's sermon 'Go Down Death', when a woman had this same question put to her as well. She told him the story of how he'd been carried from one room to another late at night, when he had fallen asleep on their bed after a long day. He had been carried from one place to another, without knowing about the journey, and had woken up the next morning in his own bed. Death, she told her son, was just like that. With this knowledge and comfort her son was no longer afraid to pass from this life to meet Jesus on the other side.

⌒

Idaho has some remarkable people that live within its borders.

In the end, for Craig and Jill, all around them did the best they could to love on this couple through this time. There was a lot of support, but what do you do as time goes on? Everyone has to go back home and get on with their lives. And so slowly the visitors, and their visits, became fewer and fewer. Though the ordeal had ended for most, for this couple it was far from over. The pain was really just beginning, as trouble slowly started to creep into their marriage and their lives and slowly began to grow.

Unlike the doctors who talked about honesty during Jesse's crisis, the counselors didn't tell them the truth. Craig and Jill had been told to wait for a year and it would start to get better. This wasn't so.

Being a man and a woman, one of the biggest problems they faced was they both grieved differently.

Craig went back to his job and buried himself in his work to alleviate the pain. There were some practical reasons for this in a way. The company he worked for had been very generous and had given him a lot of leave of absence time over the whole course of their son's sickness. In addition, many of the employees he worked with had given unselfishly during this time, donating their vacation time so Craig could be with his family during Jesse's illness. There had been so much left undone in his absence, and besides the work load, I'm sure he felt a tremendous obligation to show his gratitude to those who had given so much. It was also a bit therapeutic to bury himself in his work. He felt the need to have some distraction after Jesse's death that could be considered constructive. And unbeknownst to all he also had to insulate himself from the issues of home.

With Jill it was different – much different. Being more available she had been front and center during some crucial times in Jessie's illness – answering the death question for him and being there when Jesse's eyes closed for the last time. She needed much more continuing support than Craig did. As a mother, and a good one, her heart was broken over Jessie's loss and she needed a much longer time to heal. Looking back, it took a seemingly endless amount of time for her to cry and reflect. From my perspective the Jill that is visible to all looks better, but underneath my guess is it will be a continuing hurt until she sees him again someday. That's not counting Craig out of the equation either by the way.

Besides her wanting Jesse to somehow come back, she needed Craig to be there much more than he realized. Trouble continued to grow and eventually they split-up as a couple and parted ways.

I didn't know at the time when the split took place – but I somehow heard later that they had divorced. It was like a double blow to me, given Jesse's death and now hearing of their divorce. I cared so much about them and looked up to them both; it was saddening to me and so disheartening. After so much pain, the family was going to be destroyed too. I knew that Jessie wouldn't have wanted this to happen. He would have wanted his death to bring his mom and dad closer together – not push them apart. This was not to be.

⮑

I will always remember the next time I saw Craig. I was at a wedding years later in our small town when I saw him across the room. We made a non-verbal recognition and I was glad to see him there. When the reception ended and people were allowed to mill about, we connected again. After the preliminaries of asking how we both were doing, he had something exciting he wanted to talk with me about. He said, "Hey man, I got married again!"

I remember feeling downcast but not wanting to show it. I did my best to hide my disappointment, but I admit it was a bit of a half-hearted attempt on my part. I couldn't feign excitement when thinking of Jessie, another destroyed family and the blending of two new lives in marriage who I believed weren't really supposed to be together.

"Really? Wow," I mumbled, half-heartedly trying to make the best of it. "Congratulations. So who is she?"

"Jill – I married Jill," Craig said.

I think I told you before I'm not the fastest gun in the West. It took me a few moments to come out of the fog. I still wasn't really sure of what he said. I paused in my haze because I remembered a name much like that.

"Jill? Do you mean *Jill*?"

"Yes – Jill."

I was stunned. I was taken from grave disappointment to great joy in about 14.5 seconds. My gratitude and excitement still hasn't abated to this day.

What had happened to bring this to pass?

⌒

After the divorce Jill went back to North Dakota and Craig stayed in Idaho where his job was at. The house was split in half, the funds divided and Craig began to stay in a trailer to cut costs so he could visit his last son Hunter on a regular basis back in North Dakota. All was lost.

I will give the events to follow this in two halves.

Jill somehow had turned to alcohol in her confusion and pain, and it began to consume her life. She had been a casual drinker before, but now she drank in a way that she hoped would help her to eliminate the pain. It really didn't and never does; it just adds another demon to deal with. Rather than heal, the wound began to fester and Jill became more and more incapacitated to deal with anything. I will skip the details, because I don't know a lot of them and don't care to know, but one night, while drinking in a bar in North Dakota, Jill's transformation began to take place. Odd isn't it – the places where God will choose to meet with you when you're in trouble? As she sat at a table she began to think, "What kind of a mother am I?" It was a cry of despondency and despair to no one in general. However it was also some kind of a prayer I believe at the same time, sent upwards to God. I see her leaving that place, thinking she wasn't heard and nobody cared – but she was heard. Someone did care. God above looked down and had finally found an opening to Jill's heart. The opening was in the very place where Jill hurt the most – that place of being a good mother to her children.

For Craig I think he had taken the divorce request from Jill as simply as an answer that she had asked for. Given the circumstances in Jill's heart during this time it seemed like a closed door forever – an unresolvable issue. Craig is as honest and caring as he is pragmatic so he began to move forward, regardless of how he felt, toward the new life that had been thrust upon him. After a period of years he began to date again.

⸻

Enter my third hero, their son Hunter.

During one of these dates, his remaining son Hunter came home on one of his shared visits, to see his dad and found him entertaining a new woman. I can see this meeting in my mind, though obviously not present. Hunter pulled his dad aside at some point in the evening and asked him point blank, "Dad, what are you doing?" It is amazing to me that Hunter was in Junior High school at this time and had the courage to speak up like this.

'What are you doing' was a good question. Maybe this question, in other words, was more like, "Where are you going with your life dad and does it include us?" I think that this question should be asked more often of everyone in this circumstance, especially, in my opinion, those in Christian circles. May God give us the love and boldness to do so if the opportunity presents itself. I don't think Hunter's question was a delivered in just a question type of format – it was more like a loving inquisition from a caring son. The question Hunter raised, coupled with the love he had for his son, so impacted Craig that he called the woman the next day and called their relationship off.

There were a host of other events that began to take place but the rest is history; a marriage was restored. I've met with them several times since and it has always been a joy for me, regardless of the circumstances. The last two times we've met there were the sounds of Hunter, his wife and the grandchildren in the background. I think about how deep the impact of their combined lives has been and will continue to be.

Before you see them saddled up and riding off into a glorious sunset, there are a few things you need to know. As a good friend of mine Keev said, "Life is not always linear." What that means is everything didn't just go upward and onward for Craig and Jill like the end to a Hollywood movie.

As I sat with them on a clear Idaho day, I could see that things are way better off today than if they had stayed in the alternate scenario of a family split forever by deep and painful difficulties. All is as Jesse would have hoped for with the two of them; being together and the family unit intact. All of this came to pass but it didn't remove the continuing, severe struggle Jill had with her alcoholism. Craig did the toughest thing I've ever heard of during this time – having to turn Jill out on her own until she decided to get better. The difference was he was staying in the marriage this time but invoking a separation *for a specific purpose.*

It was such a key and critical time for Jill. Things have gotten better for her and I believe she has turned a major corner in her life – but it didn't come without a lot of heartache. What had changed for her? She told me during our last time together that she decided she doesn't want to miss any more time with her grandchildren, and will do whatever it takes to accomplish this. Again, the sweet and courageous heart of a woman who deeply loves the sound of little feet.

But there will always be Jesse's absence. Jill's emotions still run deep on this as you can guess, but Craig was much more vulnerable the last time we all talked together. Jill seemed silent in comparison, but I think it was only because she had scraped rock bottom so many times with a pick axe that there were no more spots to go any deeper. However, Craig was the most visibly broken when we were together because he talked about his distance during those times, as a husband and as a dad. I made no effort to block his feelings or compel him to refrain from saying whatever he wanted to. It was their story and a lot was still being dealt with – I was again just glad to see them dealing with it together. My admiration is not for what they will do someday in the future, it is for what they have already done now. With Jill and Craig sitting together in their home, and with Hunter, his wife and the grandchildren present in the background, I got a chance to see redemptions story all over again.

When Keev, the friend that I mentioned earlier, talked about his own rocky journey with his wife, this is when I heard the, "It's not going to be like Hollywood" thing. Keev mentioned the struggles that they've had as well, but he went on to say a very encouraging thing. "It may not be pretty at times," he said, "but there is one key thing. It's the peace and confidence of knowing, regardless of the circumstances, that you've done the right thing and that you're in the right place with God. You're doing what He would want you to be doing with your life." Words of wisdom.

There may be some issues that will trouble us forever it seems here below. But if we do the right thing, by doing what He says, putting your head on the pillow at night will not be troublesome. Knowing that you're in the center of God's will is a good place to be.

This is just one story of one family; there are many others I've heard about and been close too. But I mention these three people for they have been among the courageous and most inspiring folks I have ever known.

CHAPTER 11
My List

My List

I'm going to get a little personal here. I have my own list on who I hope to love and why.

These points I'm going to share aren't transient beliefs to me. I have found that these items on my list are like guards, keeping me from miss-understanding the difference between infatuation, a momentary strong attraction, or a possible lasting love.

This is my list – maybe you should have one of your own. I just hope your list is well thought out ahead of time and that it contains the things that you can and cannot live without.

1. **Someone whose eyes I would be willing to close in death.**

I want to love them till the end and to be there all the way for them. I don't want to lose my attraction for just wanting to be with them. If their teeth fall out, if their hearing goes bad, if their skin becomes wrinkly or their hair gets thin, I want to still love them and spend our last moments together. I believe this is what Shakespeare thought of when he penned,

Love's not Times fool, though rosy lips and cheeks within his bending sickles compass come.

Love alters not with his brief hours and weeks, but bears it out even to the edge of doom.

I want to love all the way until the end. It's important to me.

2. **Someone who is pretty and beautiful to me – inside and out.**

She may or may not look good to you – but she will always look beautiful to me. There are a sea of pretty faces but she will be captivating to me in so many other areas besides just beauty. Her intelligence for one, when coupled with her character, will definitely be important to me.

3. **Someone I would be proud of, that I would want my kids to be around.**

My daughter was frustrated with my being alone for so long and she wanted me to find another partner for life. I told her that I always thought of her and my son as an important part of the equation on the choice I'd make. I wanted to find someone that they would like as well. "Dad," she said, "don't worry about us. Whatever makes you happy is what we want too."

"Honey," I told her, "if happiness is what you want for me then good – for what would make me happy is to find someone that you would care about as well." I hope she understood.

It's a big point for me. I don't want to take someone into my life that I wouldn't be a good match for my children as well. I would want someone who would encourage them in the same directions I would and speak to them, when I am not around, about things that they don't seem to get when I open my mouth. Someone that my kids might even find 'cool' would be a blessing on top of it all.

4. **Someone that I would be willing to marry in front of everyone on the Strand.**

If you're a San Diego native, you possibly know what someone means when they talk about the 'Strand'. It's the name for the beach in front of the Hotel Del Coronado. I have lived here for years and wasn't surprised to learn recently that it is rated as one of the top 10 most beautiful beaches in the United States. It's a wonder – and you have to see it in person, along with the hotel, to experience it.

I'm not an overly demonstrative person, so outdoor weddings and lavish public ceremonies for show are not my thing. However, it would be my ideal to get married in the late afternoon on the Coronado Strand in San Diego. It's more than a beautiful and a stunning place to visit; it is also a litmus test for me. If I can't marry her here, then she's not the right one. When I think of standing in front of that seaside crowd and whoever walks buy on that boardwalk, if I wouldn't be proud enough to showcase her there, in front of everyone on the planet, then by God's grace I would just like to pass on being married at all.

Like Craig told me one time, "You've waited a long time Ken – make it good."

5.   Someone who curls my toes.

There is more to romance than just another pretty face. To me it's very attractive for a woman to have an opinion, to be a believer in Christ and to have a passion to serve Him in her life. She doesn't have to demonstrate her faith the way I do, but in her own way it is vibrant. I would hope that what she does with her life and her faith is meaningful to her and others. But with all this in place, I would still like to have someone who is wonderful to hold, who is beautiful to me. I know when you get older the fenders aren't going to be as nice as when the car was new, and the paint is going to have a few scratches on it, but when I see the model I'm looking for – the rest won't matter.

6.   Someone who won't leave me during the hard times, and vice versa.

I don't know what else to say here than this. I know that life can throw you some pretty tough curves, but I want to be faithful to her through all of this. I've struggled in the past, and my faith in God hasn't been what it should have been in so many ways, but

I want this to change. He certainly has proved Himself faithful to me over and over again. I just need patience, a little belief from her and some understanding while I work this out.

7.   I don't want a clone.

She can have different interests, have a Boston accent, hold democratic opinions and love a different baseball team – none of that matters as much to me as just loving her. We may disagree at times, but I hope we have wonderful conversations and new interests together. It may not be easy to both be different, but all I ask is that she will be someone that I will love deeply.

༄

I hope this has been helpful to you. I can't wait to see someday what you wrote down.

Ken Connelly has a heart for people and has been gifted with the abilities of an artist, author, musician and technical support person in manufacturing. He is the proud father of two good individuals, Nathan & Meghan. He works as an engineer for GKN Aerospace in San Diego, CA and is a member of Shadow Mountain Church.

Daniel Sorensen is a talented artist and illustrator. He has a Bachelor of Fine Arts Degree and Master of Fine Arts Degree, and is an active member of the Portrait Society of America and Oil Painters of America. He has exhibited his work in numerous shows around the U.S. and is the professor of painting and drawing at Odessa College in Texas, where he resides with his wife Katie and their 4 children. It is a personal pleasure to have his work within these pages.

Nicole Dudley is my Author Manager at Gatekeeper Press and I am thankful for her help in this work.

Email is: kennethconnelly53@gmail.com
Website is: http://the-forgotten-option.squarespace.com/

CPSIA information can be obtained
at www.ICGtesting.com
Printed in the USA
BVHW090632271120
594195BV00009B/31/J